Above the Mountain's Shadow

A Journey of Hope and Adventure Inspired by the Forgotten

Sara Safari and Jeffrey A. Kottler

cognella® | PRESS

Cognella Press
Published by Cognella, Inc.
Cognella, Inc., 3970 Sorrento Valley Blvd, San Diego, CA 92121

First published in the United States of America in 2018 by Cognella, Inc.

Cover design by Emely Villavicencio.

ISBN: 978-1-5165-3321-3 (pbk)

cognella® | PRESS

www.cognella.com   800-200-3908

This book is dedicated to the courageous and resilient girls and women who struggle against oppression, abuse, neglect, and exploitation. Although the focus of much of our work has been in Nepal and among refugees, both in the United States and abroad, we applaud the efforts of dedicated advocates, volunteers, and professionals who are doing their best to make a difference everywhere.

Cognella editions also by Jeffrey Kottler:

Living and Being a Therapist: A Collection of Readings

Understanding Research: Becoming a Competent and Critical Consumer

Forthcoming Cognella editions by Jeffrey Kottler:

Fallen Heroes: Tragedy, Madness, Resilience, and Inspiration among Famous Athletes

Handbook of Refugee Experience: Trauma, Resilience, and Recovery
Learning Group Leadership

Making a Difference: A Journey of Adventure, Disaster, and Redemption Inspired by the Plight of At-Risk Girls

Theories of Counseling and Psychotherapy

Authors' Note

The structure of the book is somewhat unusual in that our story includes the narrative voices of both authors—each of whom was struggling for survival in very different settings—in various chapters. The catastrophic events unfolded at the same time in different parts of the world, including the United States, Kathmandu, Mount Everest, and the epicenter of the second major earthquake that took place in the Khumbu region near Everest Base Camp.

Although all the events and experiences described in this book occurred as described, the names of some of the individuals mentioned in the story have been changed.

Sara Safari
San Diego, California

Jeffrey Kottler
Houston, Texas

Table of Contents

1

Buried

Sara
April 2015

Each breath was agonizing. I sounded like Darth Vader taking slow, deep wheezing gasps of air. Each step on the ladder required another breath, timed carefully so I could rest in between. But I knew I had to speed things up. Every moment I spent in the Khumbu Icefall was testing fate. This was the most dangerous part of the ascent to the top of Mt. Everest, the place where more people have died. I put all that out of my mind and just concentrated on the next step on the ladder. I looked up and could see I still had another 100 meters to go.

I forced myself to stop and look around and admire the beauty, certainly one of the most spectacular place on Earth with turquoise glaciers and ice towers standing vigil all around me. I tried to raise my goggles for a moment to check the colors, but the sky was so blue, and the reflected sunlight off the snow was so bright, all I could do was squint at the horizon. I thought how many people in the whole world have the opportunity to be here. I had never felt so fortunate to be and feel so alive.

I think the danger was part of the incredible exhilaration. From my view atop ladders roped together and anchored to the side of the glacier I could see the dark crevasses below. I knew that at any moment one could open up beneath me and I'd disappear forever. I shook those thoughts away and reached into my outer parka for a camera. I remembered my mother told me at the airport as she dropped me off for the long flights to Nepal that I shouldn't be distracted by taking pictures, just to concentrate on staying safe. But I had to capture this magic moment. The utter stillness.

After removing my mittens for the photos my fingers felt numb. They had already been stiff after five hours climbing ladders and walking across gaping caverns in the ice. I needed to remember to wear warmer liners under my gloves when we arrived at Camp One in another hour. This was on the South Col, the shoulder of the mountain halfway to the South Ridge at 20,000 feet. I'd been higher before on previous climbs but never one with so many of these ladders across wide crevasses and up steep cliffs.

I tried to gather my energy again for the final climb. More deep, ragged breaths. Then I could hear Damian, one of the expedition guides, yelling up to me. "Get going, Sara! This part is wickedly dangerous. We all need to get off these ladders and onto safer ground."

I nodded but felt paralyzed. I knew this was our last wall for the day, but I was exhausted and terrified.

"Come on, girl!" Damian yelled again. "Get a move on it."

I could feel calmness taking over. The breathing seemed to help, as did remembering all my training. For months, for years, maybe all my life I'd been preparing for this ladder. But I'd already climbed over, across, and up 50 ladders on this expedition. Why did *this* one seem so different? Was there some premonition? Was something, some memory triggering me?

As I slowly proceeded upward, one clanging step of my crampons at a time, I felt some abrupt movement on the ladder and then I was immediately flooded by an intensely familiar feeling, one that seemed to overwhelm me. It's like I was transported back in time to my childhood in Iran. I had this vivid image of climbing a fig tree near our home and my grandfather was shaking the branches back and forth, just like I felt right now. "Get down here!" he yelled at me. "Don't you know girls don't climb trees?"

It was almost as if it was Damian's voice I heard say those words. But before I could sort that out I became suddenly aware that the ladder I was clutching was now swinging back and forth like the fig tree from the past. But then I studied the wall in front of me and saw clearly that a few of the studs had pulled out but the ladder was still partially attached. It wasn't just the ladder that was moving—it was the whole world.

I tried to scream for help but there was no air. People were yelling at me, telling me what to do, but their voices were muffled. I heard the words, "earthquake," and "avalanche" but they didn't make sense. It was as if I lost the ability to understand English altogether. My brain seemed to shut down.

I could feel ferocious wind and a blizzard of snow threatening to blow me off the ladder that was now swinging wildly out of control. I could hear cracking ice and saw huge chunks of the wall breaking off around me. The ice towers were collapsing like buildings that had imploded. I knew in seconds I was going to be buried and there seemed to be nothing I could do to stop it.

"Cover your mouth! Cover your mouth!" I could now hear Damian screaming. I realized he was telling me the avalanche was coming. Forget my mouth, I was thinking. I have to get off this ladder. I scrambled upward as fast as I could, fighting against the blowing wind and snow. As soon as I crested the top I clipped my myself to an anchor with all the carabiners in my possession. I knew this was futile and there was no way I could hold on with the force of the avalanche that was coming. I kicked my crampons deep into the ice, buried my head into the snow, and held onto the ropes with all my strength. I could no longer feel my fingers at all and my breathing was so panicked I was on the verge of hyperventilating.

One of my last thoughts was wondering if they'd ever find my body. And then as the snow covered me I thought of that fig tree back home and all the warnings I'd been given that girls just didn't do this sort of thing.

Going Beyond Myself

Sara
October 2012

It has been over fifteen years since my family and I first moved to the United States from Iran. It was a time of great turmoil. Yes, I know there *always* seems to be a certain amount of turbulence in that part of the world: nations feuding with one another, Sunnis versus Shia, clergy versus royal families—it seems never-ending. We managed to escape the chaos to make a better life for ourselves the way so many other immigrants came to the United States for sanctuary and better opportunities.

There had been a series of student protests against the Iranian government's crackdown on more freedoms, leading to the arrest of more than four thousand people, with dozens of others murdered in the streets or tortured in dungeons. During this time, I was a student studying at university in Tehran, and I tried to remain as invisible as possible. Growing up, I'd witnessed women trying to avoid the spotlight, reluctant to ever speak their minds. My mother never had a voice, never expressed any opinions, never did or said anything that would draw attention. I found this both curious and disturbing.

At this point, my family had been waiting thirteen years for visas to leave the country, and I didn't want to take the risk that anything I might do would ruin our chances for escape. I had been arrested a few times, once because the skin on my arm was showing after I rolled up the sleeves of my dress, and the second time because I had been studying with a male student to whom I wasn't married.

I lived in constant fear of getting in trouble. My family was not religious nor particularly observant, but ever since I was a child, I'd been told over and over again at school that a girl would go to hell if she did not always cover herself. Women had to ask men permission for everything—to work, to drive a car, to go for a walk unaccompanied, and especially to ever leave the country, which was my dream. Although I was studying engineering, I knew that I'd never have the opportunity to work as a real professional in Iran; my parents approved of my studies because they thought it would make me more independent, a sentiment not common in Iranian households.

Once we were finally granted permission to leave Iran after so many years of pleading and applications, I started dreaming about America and all the things I would be allowed to do there that I could never do at home. Although my parents and siblings settled in Arizona, I had always wanted to attend the University of California, Los Angeles to study electrical engineering. I had heard the word "UCLA" many times amongst the smartest students at my university in Tehran, so it seemed like no less a "magical kingdom" than Disneyland.

When we landed at the Los Angeles airport, I thought I had arrived in a small village. There was little traffic compared to the chaos of Tehran, no pollution (relatively speaking), no pedestrians in the streets. *Where* was *everyone?* I wondered. The few pedestrians I spied were wearing shorts, like they were going to the beach or on holiday. There were a lot of palm trees like I'd seen in the movies and green spaces that didn't appear to be occupied. I also noticed that everyone on the freeway was staying in their lanes, always looking forward but not honking their horns all the time like they do at home. I had been living in a crowded city my whole life, and now I felt so alone with all the relative quiet.

The most amazing thing of all was that once I got out of the car and walked across the street, they had these magic spaces called crosswalks that no cars could enter, at least while I was inside the lines. This one driver just stopped abruptly and waited politely for me to get to the other side before he proceeded. This was incredible! I had to test this because in Iran, nobody ever stops for anyone, and it is like being in a combat zone. I crossed the street back and forth three more times, and the same exact thing happened. It was amazing.

Once I arrived on campus, I thought it was the most beautiful place I'd ever seen, with its brick buildings, diversity of students, and the highest academic standards. The students were so many different colors and spoke so many languages. I'd never seen anything like this. I applied and was accepted; however, I discovered I was not prepared for the many adjustments I would have to make to reach my goal.

First of all, the university wouldn't accept any of my three previous years of study, so I had to start my education over again. Secondly, I had learned English in Tehran with a British accent, and people sometimes had a hard time understanding me, as I did them. The customs were so different too. In the Persian culture, it is common for girls to hold hands when they walk around, but I remember reaching for another student's hand as we were strolling to class, and she pulled away, accusing me of being a lesbian. In addition, students spent so much time in bars, and I hadn't yet ever tasted alcohol. Girls wore tank tops, shorts, and revealing clothes, another thing to which I was unaccustomed.

My apartment at UCLA was tiny, basically just a small room. The building was so old that I couldn't close the windows, which was a problem, considering that my neighbors partied a lot. I had to use earplugs just to be able to sleep at night, and I had to study in the library because there was no way to concentrate at home with music blaring at all hours. I had never been around people who drank so much and partied all the time; back in Iran, none of this is allowed, so I was unequipped to deal with this strange behavior.

Throughout my time at UCLA, I worked hard to achieve the highest grades, not only to make my family proud but also so I could build a good life for myself. It was all about wanting things that I could never have back in Iran. I wanted to be able to support myself without depending on a man. I wanted a nice car. I wanted a house of my own. I wanted a husband, eventually—and maybe a few kids. It was all about wanting, without almost any thought about what would truly make me happy. I could earn the best grades, get the best job, maybe even become a professor and teach engineering, but I started to wonder if that was what would really make me feel satisfied.

When I reflected more deeply, I realized that I didn't know what I wanted most. I had never really been permitted to have any grandiose dreams—not atypical for an Iranian woman. I realized that the things I thought I wanted most were related to a small, selfish life benefitting only myself and my family. Sure, I wanted to be able to support myself someday and help my family, but I also wanted to make my mark in the world, to do something *useful* that would help many others.

I worked so hard that first semester to prove myself, to show my family—and myself—that I could succeed in this very different country. This was a place where women like me were not only allowed to work but were actually encouraged to get an education. And yet I remember that after surviving my first semester and completing my exams, the thought hit me that maybe this was it, that I'd already gone as far as I could go. My mood plummeted, and I wondered if perhaps there was something more to life than this, more than just academic achievement and material success.

I'd always been good at math, science, and technical subjects—unusual for a girl from Iran, where such opportunities are very limited. I wanted to break this mold, to prove that women really could do almost anything men could do. But I wanted more for my life than sitting in a laboratory designing and testing circuit boards to optimize their speed and power usage.

Hiding Under the Table

My father used to terrify me—and everyone else in the household. He was an angry and unhappy man who decided to make everyone else miserable to keep him company. I remember when I was about nine years old, playing outside the house with my friends. One of them abruptly asked me why my last name was different from my father's. I was not only taken aback by the question but also shocked that I'd never considered it before myself. I didn't realize that it was important or even something to notice. I just thought that my last name was chosen by my parents because "Safari" goes so well with "Sara."

"No, stupid," my friend laughed, "you are like me."

"Of course I'm like you," I said, confused by her point. "That's why we're friends!"

"Sara, you lost your dad in the war with Iraq, and then your mom got married again. Just like what happened to me."

I just shook my head and walked away. I couldn't believe what she was saying. I thought she was lying or trying to hurt me, especially when she announced that my sister wasn't my "real" sister and that I was lucky to just be able to live with her. I was just confused. Why did my mother marry someone else? Wasn't I enough for her?

On some level, this started to make sense to me—why my father and his mother were so mean to me all the time. My father's mother would complain about me all the time. I remember hoping that someday my father might love me like a daughter if I acted better or tried harder.

One day when I was six years old, I was playing under the dining room table, crawling over the chairs and climbing between them. I had carefully arranged all my dolls and stuffed animals on a blanket beside the table, covering them with another blanket while they took an afternoon nap. Some of my other toys were scattered around the floor.

I heard the front door creak open and then slam shut so hard I could feel the vibrations. "Nasim," I heard my father yell at my mother, "what the hell is going on around here? The house is a mess. What were you doing all day while I've been working so hard?"

My mother was in the kitchen preparing dinner, so she didn't get the full brunt of his rage. But *I* did while cowering under the table, fearful he would beat me.

"I'm sorry, Babak," my mother said, wiping her hands on a towel. "I didn't know you were coming home so early."

"This house is not clean! It's a mess. Look at all the shit around here," he said, pointing to my stuff scattered on the floor. I was still hiding in the shadow of the table.

"Babak," my mother tried to explain, "I was just—"

I heard a loud smack and saw my mother fall to the floor after he'd hit her. She started crying, and then he walked outside to smoke a cigarette. My mother could see me under the table, and that made her even more fearful. "Quick, run to the public phone and tell your uncle to come quickly. Otherwise, I … I don't know—"

I nodded my head in understanding, and my mother placed a small coin in my hand to make the call. She repeated my uncle's phone number several times so I could repeat it back to her. Then I ran as fast as I could out the door, hoping my father would not catch me.

Because I was so little, I had to climb up to reach the phone booth. I could barely grasp the phone, so when I tried to put the coin in the slot, it got stuck, and I couldn't push it in. I was just so scared that something would happen to my mother while I was away that all I could think to do was rush home to try and save her.

My mother was still huddled on the floor a few minutes later, holding her hand to the side of her face. The memories of this day are all muddled together because they merge with so many others just like it, when we all lived in fear of my father's temper.

Only once, after a beating, did I finally yell, "Why do you hurt me? What did I ever do to you that you hate me so much?"

He looked at me, really seemed to *see* me, and just shrugged and shook his head. "Sometimes," he said in an uncharacteristically quiet voice, "I just get so angry I can't control myself. I don't know what I'm doing."

I really did believe it was my fault that he was so unhappy and abusive at times. He had such a hard life. And I must have felt like another burden to him.

We all understood that he'd lived through some very difficult times, and, strangely, I could never bring myself to blame him for scaring me so much.

It just made me determined to never allow a man to control my life when I got older.

My mother had always told me that education was the way out of this trap. Education was equal to freedom for me, a way out of the entrapment. Any time I would complain, she would tell me that the best way to fight back was to study and do my best in school so I could have different opportunities. That was the way I could earn my independence and make my own choices for the future. To so many girls in this part of the world, education was the only way out—but an opportunity completely closed to them.

Beyond the Impossible

After I graduated from UCLA, I immediately got a job as a test engineer working on power management systems for mobile phones and software for autopilot systems in airplanes. I was now a professional engineer. But I still didn't feel satisfied. I had completed my education, my way to independence—so why wasn't it enough?

Choosing science and engineering as my fields of study had limited my exposure to so many other aspects of life about which I was completely unaware, especially in this new country where the rules for success were so different. Compared to American students, I lacked so much confidence. I was shy and reluctant to take any risks or venture outside of what felt comfortable. I also felt so burdened by my past struggles and traumatic experiences. I could feel myself becoming increasingly angry and resentful; things were not improving as I had hoped.

I signed up for a series of leadership seminars, hoping to improve my confidence, if not my self-esteem. During one of the first meetings, we were required to make a commitment to—and a public declaration of—an ambitious goal that would be transformative for our lives. The instructor told us that it was only by creating ambitious goals that we could go far beyond what we ever imagined was possible. "I want you to reach for something big," he said, "something so huge that it might seem impossible."

Frankly, nothing immediately came to mind; I just sat there feeling stuck. In order to fulfill a dream, first you have to have one, and I was drawing a complete blank. First, I thought about taking a dance or painting class; nope, too easy. Then I considered going on for a doctorate in electrical engineering;

that was harder, for sure, but it wasn't something that seemed out of reach, since I'd been working hard to excel in my studies my whole life.

I always wanted to open a wellness center, but that didn't seem that impossible either. I needed to think of something truly spectacular, something that seemed completely outlandish. I wanted to make a statement, not just to those in attendance but to myself.

I could hear echoes of conversation as other participants were talking to one another about their plans. Behind me, I could hear two people talking. "I think I'm going to go trekking in Nepal."

"Trekking in Nepal?" the other one asked and started giggling. "Isn't that kind of dangerous? I mean, they've got avalanches, and I think there's some kind of civil war going on."

"No, seriously, my friend went trekking in the Himalayas and went all the way to Everest Base Camp. She said it was amazing. It was really hard but totally worth it."

And in that moment, I thought to myself, *That's it! But I'm not going to just trek to Base Camp; I'm going to climb Mount Everest, the highest mountain in the world!* Before I could stop myself, I blurted out my plan to the group. I felt giddy with the power of my declaration.

Of course, what made this utterly ridiculous is that I'd never been climbing, or even hiking, in my life. I was always very little and quite skinny, a hungry waif who looked like a strong wind could knock me over. Back in Tehran, about the only exercise I ever got was running behind my mother to catch a bus or taxi or playing hide-and-seek with my friends. I refused to even visit the park because I much preferred walking on asphalt. To make matters even more improbable, I'd never been camping before and didn't really like the outdoors.

If my lack of experience in nature wasn't enough of an obstacle, I absolutely hated cold weather. Even in Southern California, land of eternal sunshine, I would complain whenever the temperature dipped below seventy degrees. I'd also never been on a real mountain before, and even the prospect of snow was somewhat of a mystery to me.

I didn't own a single piece of clothing or equipment that would be appropriate for such an adventure. If our leader truly wanted us to pick something that was beyond impossible, I sure delivered that. But *now* what was I going to do? I looked around the room with everyone staring at me, but now I couldn't let them down. They actually expected me to *do* this.

Instruction Manual for Climbing Everest

Sara
December 2012

If I thought I had gotten some strange looks when I announced my plan to those at the seminar, I hadn't anticipated the reactions I'd get from my family and friends when I told them what I had in mind. Everything that I had done so far in my life was the result of someone else's influence or preferences. It felt like all of my life decisions had been made by others, whether controlled by the authoritarian government and religious leaders in Iran, the demands of my parents, or the expectations of what was considered appropriate for an Iranian girl. I just couldn't stand the idea any longer of someone, *anyone*, trying to control me. I didn't need a man in my life to feel worthy. I wanted to do things that had previously been prohibited: wearing different clothes, enjoying a little alcohol, being overtly affectionate with a guy. I wanted to show everyone—and most of all, myself—that I was far from being that help-less girl any longer. To me, Everest represented something more than just a mountain to be conquered: it was the embodiment of all that I'd been told was out of my reach.

I tried to explain all of this to my friends, but I never felt like anyone really understood what I was doing and why I was doing it.

"That's pretty funny," one friend said, thinking I was kidding when I told him about my plans. "So, what you doing this weekend?"

"I just told you what I'm doing, and you just ignored me."

He just laughed. "You idiot! Climbing mountains is for rich people."

I didn't tell my family at all because I knew that would be a hopeless cause leading to only more grief and discouragement. I had now been married for a few years, and my husband, Matt, thought this was just a passing fad that would eventually run its course; his best strategy was just to indulge me. I couldn't exactly disagree with him, considering that I had already learned on the Internet that the climb itself would take two months, and I couldn't imagine living in the cold for more than a few hours. So I decided to keep it all a secret, a skill that I'd been trained to do from the earliest age.

Okay, so maybe I would have reacted much the same way if someone without any experience, training, or even any previous interest in mountaineering all of a sudden proclaimed she was going to attempt one of the most difficult and dangerous climbs in the world. The first thing I had done when I got home was to Google "How to climb Mount Everest," as if there would be instructions I could follow. After all, I'm a computer geek and engineer; I'm pretty good at following directions.

The most distressing thing I learned was that something like one in ten climbers who attempt the summit end up dying in the process. Hmmm. That wasn't very encouraging. I read further to discover there were hundreds of bodies still frozen up there that they couldn't pry loose from the ice as well as various body parts and artifacts of those who had tried to get to the top and failed.

I'm not one to be dissuaded easily—some have called me stubborn. Any time my parents told me I couldn't do something—cross the busy street near our apartment, play boys games in the street—I defied them and did exactly the opposite. I was told over and over that girls weren't supposed to climb trees or go very high on the swings at the playground. Each warning just served to motivate me. Those closest to me knew quite well that they would be better off just not saying anything at all rather than trying to talk me out of my plan; they knew it would only make me more determined to prove them wrong.

During my initial search for information about how to climb Everest, I noticed that one company was mentioned frequently as one of the major expedition leaders, so I decided to call them on the phone.

"Good morning, Alpine Climbing."

"Hi. I have a question for you."

"Yes, of course."

"How do I climb Mount Everest?"

"Let me transfer you. Please hold."

As I was waiting, I could feel my heart pounding. I couldn't believe I was actually doing this—or even *thinking* about doing this.

"So," another voice came on the line, this time a guy who, I assumed, was one of their guides. "I understand you are interested in one of our Everest expeditions."

"Yes, so what can you tell me, and what do I need to do?"

"Well, first of all, tell me about your previous climbing experience."

"My climbing experience?"

"Yeah. Which 6,000-meter summits have you already done?"

I did the math in my head. Six thousand meters was over 19,000 feet—19,685, to be precise. And I guess he wasn't referring to the time I had spent at high altitude in an airplane. "Well," I admitted right away, "actually, I've never been climbing before."

I could hear the guy laughing, and it made me angry.

"All right then, why don't you start with Mount Whitney? It's in California. The highest peak in the continental United States. You can do it as a day hike. Try that and then maybe give us a call back."

Click.

If this guide thought he was discouraging me, he was wrong. Now I had a place to begin. I was so excited that I immediately started reading about Whitney and how to climb it, which routes were possible, and what equipment I'd need. I read about people's experiences on their blogs and in their comments and realized that this would be a lot more than a stroll in the park. But still, it was *only* 14,500 feet, and Everest was literally *double* that height. So how hard could it be?

Perhaps I should mention that this was in the middle of winter, and there would likely be tons of snow on the mountain. Almost everyone who attempts the summit waits until the middle of July, when the trails are clear, but there was no way I was going to wait to put my plan into action. *Besides,* I was thinking, *there's snow on Everest, isn't there?* This would be even better training for the real thing.

The next day, I showed up at the local sporting goods store and walked up to the first salesperson I could find, a young guy with shoulder-length hair and a full beard. He looked like the kind of person who might know a thing or two about climbing mountains. "Excuse me, I was wondering—I mean, I have a question."

He looked up from folding fleece sweaters on a table, obviously a little annoyed with my interruption, but he quickly recovered and remembered to smile. "Sure, what can I help you find?"

"Well," I explained, all in a rush, "I'm planning on climbing Mount Whitney in a few weeks. I don't have any gear for something like that, and I was wondering if you could help me."

"You want to climb Whitney?"

I nodded.

"Now? You want to climb Whitney *now*?"

"Uh-huh." I gave him my best smile.

"You do know it's winter this time of year? The temperature is like, below zero, with thirty-mile-per-hour winds. And snow. Lots of snow. Probably ten feet of snow in places."

"That's perfect," I answered. "Because I'm planning on climbing Everest, so this will be similar conditions."

"Lady, that's just not possible. Is this a joke or something?" Now I was becoming more than a little annoyed. Nobody was taking me seriously. Even my closest friends believed that once I tried this out a few times, I'd come to my senses and do something else. It bothered me once again that someone, anyone, was telling me I couldn't do something. How dare they! I think the salesman saw that determined look in my eyes and backed off.

"Okay, okay," he said, holding his hand out in a gesture of a surrender after having spent ten minutes telling me all the reasons why I couldn't and shouldn't attempt such a stupid thing. "I'll tell you what you'd need for something like this, but I've got to warn you, what you're thinking about is really dangerous. I've been climbing for a lot of years, and I'd never attempt a climb like this during the winter."

The baskets in the store were too small for everything I'd need, so we found a shopping cart and filled it to the brim with a lot more stuff than I could possibly have anticipated—wool underwear, fleece tops, layers of clothing, boots, crampons, gloves, face mask, and a waterproof, breathable shell jacket that was insanely expensive. We added a backpack, water bottles, a sleeping bag and pad, water purifier, and all kinds of other stuff. "Oh yeah, you'll need a pair of sunglasses."

"Got those already," I said with a grin, pointing to the pair perched on my head.

He shook his head with worry. "Look, lady. Even though it's winter, the sun is intense and reflects off the snow. It will burn you to a crisp and probably give you snow blindness." When he saw my confused look, he explained, "You need polarized glacier glasses to protect your eyes." Again, he just shook his head. I had to be the most memorable customer he'd seen in a long time.

Once I had all the equipment and supplies organized and assembled, my next task was to begin training. So I filled up my new backpack with all the stuff, added a few books in there for more weight, and headed off to the gym to start walking on a treadmill. This wasn't as simple as I thought: the fitness facility wouldn't let me into the place with my pack.

"We have rules against this sort of thing."

"Against *what* sort of thing?" I asked. The receptionist wouldn't budge, so I had to join another fitness club that had a more relaxed policy.

I was surprised that walking with the pack was so difficult—it was much heavier than I thought it would be—and several times, I almost fell over backwards. It seemed that I had some balancing issues to work on, because I found it difficult to even stand upright with all the weight.

It occurred to me that mountaineering expeditions always have teams of climbers who work together, so I needed to recruit my own members. I started calling everyone I knew to invite them to go with me on my expedition, starting with my best friend, Pari.

"Ah, gee, thanks for the invitation," she answered without hesitation. "But I *definitely* have plans that weekend."

"But I didn't mention which weekend we were going yet. I just told you I was going to do this and asked if you would go with me."

"Okay, then, you're right," Pari begged off. "But this kind of thing just isn't my thing, if you know what I mean."

This surprised me because Pari was always game for whatever scheme I had in mind. In some ways, she was a major source of inspiration for me because she was in the process of reinventing her own life by attending a graduate program in counseling. She would go on and on about a professor of hers, Dr. Kottler, who she mentioned also spent some time in the Himalayas. She had traveled with his team of volunteers the previous year, and showed me endless photos of the children they were helping, all girls whose lives were in jeopardy.

But I guess it did seem a little outlandish to ask my friends to climb the highest peak in the country—in the winter—without any prior experience. But I'd seen photos of people at the summit, and some of them didn't look like they were in particularly good shape. How hard could it be?

Finally, one of my friends mentioned someone he knew, Mo, who was an experienced climber. Maybe he'd go with me? I could tell he was just trying to get me off his back, but I appreciated the gesture. So I called Mo, and he accepted my invitation—my first team member! "Sure," he agreed, "I'll go with you. I totally support you all the way to the top of Everest." He even assembled a group of his climbing friends who would join us to climb to the top of Whitney.

It was the middle of December when we prepared to leave. I tried my pack on after loading it with all my stuff, noting that it seemed a *lot* heavier than when I had been practicing on a treadmill. That's the first time I considered that this adventure might be a little over my head. Those creeping thoughts became a lot more than a whisper when we first started up the trail in the deep snow. I hadn't slept the night before at our starting point, which was already at 10,000 feet. As I've already mentioned, I'd never been camping before.

My heart was pounding in my chest from the altitude, and that scared me. I kept hearing noises in the middle of the night that I thought might be bears threatening to eat me (I didn't even realize, at that point, that bears hibernate in the winter). The worst part of all was pooping and peeing in the wilderness. Being a woman from the Middle East, I wasn't exactly prepared for going to the toilet "in public," and I was too scared to wander too far into the woods because I was afraid that something might eat me.

To make matters worse, Mo had a bad headache and nausea from the altitude, and we hadn't even started climbing yet. I was incredibly disappointed that we'd come this far and now had to turn back before we even started. I told Mo to wait for me so I could at least go a little bit up the trail. Once I was alone, I started to talk to the mountain. "Hello, there, Whitney," I began, feeling more than a little foolish. "I just want to let you know that I have to leave now." I stopped to look up at where I thought the summit might be. "But I promise I'm coming back. Real soon."

I was extremely frustrated that my first mountaineering experience took the form of basically just peeing in the woods. But hey, you've got to start somewhere.

It took two more months before I could convince anyone else to go with me, and I knew it wasn't the sort of thing I could do alone for the first time. It was the middle of February, even colder than before, when another friend and I prepared to make the trip. And this time I was absolutely determined to get to the top, no matter what. I'd already lost time in my planned training schedule. Unfortunately, at the very last moment, my friend backed out, saying he had to take care of some business. I don't know if I believed him or not, but it didn't matter—I was going on my own.

A Nudge from the Universe

The morning of the climb, I woke up to a huge snowfall. The road in and out of the Whitney trailhead was closed, but I still wouldn't let that stop me. I continued on in my car, slipping and sliding until I ended up stuck in a ditch. Foiled again! I was in the middle of nowhere, with no chance of anyone around to help me. So you can imagine my surprise when two guys walked up to me, wondering what the hell I was doing out there in the middle of winter. When I told them I was on my way to climb Whitney, they just nodded their heads like that made perfect sense and proceeded to push me out of the ditch to continue on my way. It's like they were angels sent to help and support me. I still believe that when you want something badly enough, when there's something you just *have* to do, the forces of the universe show up to give you a nudge. In my case, quite literally.

Once I arrived at the trailhead, I looked around and noticed that not only was I the only human inhabitant in the vicinity, but from the appearance of the snow-covered landscape, it didn't look like anyone had been around for a while.

I geared up and settled the backpack on my shoulders—loaded with all my supplies, and two liters of water—and started up before I got too cold. Maybe that's why I immediately developed leg cramps. I thought that maybe that was a sign, a warning, that I should turn around, but I realized that if I gave up then, my whole plan would collapse.

It had taken a solid hour just to walk from the car to the trailhead in the deep snow. With every step, I'd sink up to my thighs, so I worried I might get stuck and not be able to move. I was also concerned that all the streams were frozen, leading me to wonder how I'd replenish my water supply. It was eerily quiet—not a sound except my labored breathing.

The whole world was white. Huge piles of heavy snow buried trees with just a few branches sticking out. As I marched up the slope, lifting my legs as high as I could, I heard cracking sounds from underneath the drifts, as if the trees were crying out for help. I kept worrying about bears, wondering if one might wake up from his nap and ambush me. Even once I got moving again, it was still bitterly cold, the sun not yet visible beyond the peaks that surrounded me. I kept reminding myself that this "little" mountain was just half the size of Everest—no big deal.

I tried humming or singing to myself just to keep myself company. I was reluctant to put on my headphones and listen to music because I wanted to remain alert in case an animal tried to sneak up on me. "You got this," I kept telling myself over and over like a mantra. "I'm okay. I can do this."

But already, I was hearing whispers of doubt. The backpack was unbearably heavy. My feet felt like they were attached to iron weights from having to lift my legs so high, cutting my own trail. At least I *hoped* this was the trail. That's another thing that frightened me: I wasn't even sure I was headed along the right path to get to the top.

I forced myself to continue upward, and after another mile or two, my muscles settled into an almost comfortable cadence. I climbed and climbed all day long, finally reaching a spot to set up camp for the night just as it started to get dark. It was getting really cold now that the sun had fallen behind the mountains, and I was losing visibility. The whole landscape was blanketed with snow. The only relatively dry spot I could find to pitch my tent was on top of a flat rock that was slightly tilted.

The next order of business was to resupply my water, since I had finished the two liters on the way up and I knew the only way to stave off altitude sickness was to keep myself hydrated (the sporting goods sales guy kept telling me that over and over). After laying out all my gear and arranging my sleeping bag, I trounced down to the lake below me, which was frozen solid. It was a good thing I had an ice axe with me, wasn't it?

I chopped a hole in the ice large enough to slip the bottles underneath to refill them, feeling my hand freezing instantly from the bitter cold. As I walked back to my camp, I kept flexing my fingers over and over to regain some measure of circulation. It occurred to me that the bottles of water themselves would likely freeze in these temperatures within hours if I didn't take precautions, so I put both of them at the bottom of my sleeping bag, knowing my body heat would keep them in a relatively liquid state.

Which isn't true at all. I learned that much, much later. But at this point, all I could think about was that there was no way I wanted to leave my sleeping bag during the night. I figured that keeping them in my bag would be much more convenient. It was an excellent idea, except for one little thing—it turned out that my hands were so numb after I extricated them from the frozen lake that I didn't completely screw the top back onto one of the bottles, which proceeded to drench my bag. I reached inside the bag to try and take the leaking bottle out, and in so doing, I stepped on my sleeping pad, making a hole in it, and it immediately flattened.

Oh, did I happen to mention that I had decided *not* to bring a tent with me in order to save some weight in my bag? So here I was, sitting on a rock on top of a wet sleeping bag, with the temperature plummeting and the wind starting to blow furiously. I wasn't sure if I was shaking because of the bitter cold or my own terror, knowing that I was in deep, deep trouble. "So," I said to myself out loud, "*this* is how people die out here." Then I burst into tears, huddling myself into a ball.

I sat there sobbing for about twenty minutes, eventually waking from my stupor when the wind started kicking up snow into my face. I didn't seem to have much time left, so I crawled inside my wet sleeping bag, which was only a little better than moving from a freezer into a refrigerator. I took out my phone and turned on the video to record my last words.

"I'm so, so sorry. So sorry. I shouldn't have come here. I shouldn't be here alone. Everyone was right. I have no business doing this. Not—not—just not a good idea. But too late. I wish—I wish I didn't do this. I wish—"

And then a funny thing happened. It's like my brain got plugged back in or something. I could hear this voice talking to me, saying, "You don't have to die here."

I forced myself to close my eyes and take a few deep, frigid breaths. And then I started talking to myself in a firm voice: "Okay, first thing, you've got to stay hydrated. Better to eat something too. Need calories. Energy. Got to keep moving. Stay warm. Find shelter."

I wondered if I should try to build an igloo, dig a snow shelter. Good idea. But number one, I didn't have a shovel. And number two, I was too cold and exhausted to do anything except collapse to the ground. "This is not good," I muttered over and over as I noticed that night was descending and it was now quite dark.

All My Fears

All of a sudden, the stuff I'd been reading about mountaineering came back to me. "First of all, I've got to quit whining. Then I've got to get some food in me right away and start moving to get some heat back into my body before it's too late." It took more than two hours of running in place to get some feeling back into my limbs. By this time, I needed to rest, having spent the previous nine hours climbing. I kept telling myself, "Don't fall asleep, don't fall asleep," or I knew it would be all over for me. I had to try and stay awake all night or I'd freeze to death for sure in the frigid bag that was sopping wet.

I must have dozed off, because about two in the morning, I felt someone— or something—touching my bag. "It's a bear!" I screamed immediately, burrowing deeper into my bag and covering my head. I read somewhere that if it was a bear, it's a good idea to play dead, so that was going to be my strategy. Once again, I forgot that every bear in this part of the world was sound asleep in its den, and would be for a few more months. I also considered that it might be someone about to rob or hurt me, or worse. But I also wondered if maybe it was someone trying to save me, so I thought it might be worth a peek.

I slowly and cautiously stuck my head outside to look around and discovered that a huge pile of snow had fallen on top of me, apparently blown by the wind. After that, there was no chance I would fall asleep, so I lay shivering, counting the minutes until dawn when I could get moving again.

When I caught the first glimmers of light in the sky, I'd never felt more relieved—I survived! I'm alive! I couldn't believe I had made it through the night. I wiggled out of my bag, which had become a crust of ice and snow, threw everything I could into it, reattached my crampons for the slippery slope, and headed down as fast as I could run.

It was in the middle of a loping, uncontrolled sprint downward that I wasn't sure which way to go. My footsteps from the day before were now completely covered in snow. The landmarks all looked different. Of course an experienced climber, or even a normal one, would have thought to bring a GPS navigation system, or at least a map, but I had just assumed I'd be following a marked trail. I kept taking wrong turns, ending up at a dead-end cliff or high ridge, and then I had to backtrack.

Then I got stuck. For a change, I had been making good progress in the likely correct direction when, without warning, I fell into a deep hole. I could feel my crampons wedged into something below me, and I couldn't move. I was buried up to my chest in what felt like a snowy grave.

I kept pushing and pulling frantically to try to wiggle out of the hole until I felt a sharp pain. It was like the mountain was holding on to me, not willing to let me go. I had to try another strategy, so I pulled off my backpack and used my hands to start digging around me, widening the hole. It took about a half hour of strenuous digging, my hands now completely frozen, until I could get to the bottom of the pit and free my boots and crampons wedged between the rocks.

I was now completely exhausted but still determined to keep going. I ramped up my speed downward, loping through the snow, continuing to take wrong turns, backtracking my steps, and starting over again. A few more times I got stuck in waist-deep snow and had to dig myself out once again. But I didn't care about any of those things; I was just so happy to be alive. By the time I got back to my car, my only thought was to get back down the mountain as fast as I could.

That night on Whitney, I had faced three of my biggest terrors: the fear of being alone, fear of the dark, and fear of the cold. Oh yeah, one more biggie—fear of death. I always thought I couldn't handle those things, even if I could deal with almost anything else. Now I was reborn. Even though I twice failed to reach the Whitney summit, I still felt I'd achieved an amazing victory just to survive, realizing I could rely on myself to get out of trouble if I needed to.

So, What's Next?

As good as I felt about my survival skills under pressure, I still felt some unfinished business: getting to the top of the damn mountain one way or the other. I waited until the spring thaw and finally reached the summit a few months later. As soon as I got back down, I immediately called Alpine Climbing, and this time when the guy answered the phone, I told him, "Okay, I climbed Whitney like you told me to. What's next?"

Rather than brushing me off, this time the guide could tell I was completely serious about my plans. "Okay, that's a start. Next you've got to take some mountaineering courses and learn proper technique."

"Yeah? Like what?" I was curious what he had in mind for me.

"You have to learn *everything!* Your life is at stake. And so are the other team members' lives who accompany you. If you do something stupid or make a thoughtless mistake, it isn't just your life you are putting in jeopardy but also the lives of those who are roped to you. One false move, and you can take everyone else down with you. We'll teach you proper technique, safety procedures. You need to learn about climbing equipment, route finding and navigation, glacier travel, climbing protection, rock climbing, steep snow, and ice climbing."

"Okay."

"Wait, I'm not done. Plus how to read glacier conditions, complete gear evaluations, conduct critical decision-making, recognize white-out conditions. . .—"

"Okay, so there's a lot—"

"—then there's crevasse rescue—"

"Crevasse? What's a crevasse?" I interrupted again.

"It's a very, very deep crack in a glacier that can appear to have no bottom. If you fall into one of those suckers, you could end up on the other side of the world."

I laughed, but he ignored the interruption and just continued. "Then there's rope and belay techniques, rappelling, cramponing, rock climbing, and self-arrest."

I kept saying, "Uh-huh," after each one on the list, afraid to display my further ignorance. Self-arrest? It sounded like I was supposed to arrest myself for some crime. But I later learned that refers to using your ice axe to stop yourself from falling off the mountain when you lose control and start slipping down an icy slope.

"Oh, and one more thing," he added.

"Yeah?" I was feeling overwhelmed at this point and really didn't want to hear "one more thing." But I tried to be polite.

"If you do end up climbing an 8,000-meter peak—that's over 26,000 feet— you'll be expected to carry your own pack. On Mount Rainier, that's about sixty-five pounds; on Denali in Alaska, much more—eighty-five pounds. Is that clear?"

"Sure," I answered, not at all sure. "But I only weigh 110 pounds."

"Then you'd better gain some weight and train more."

"But is it possible for someone my size to do this?"

He ignored the question, and I wasn't sure what that meant, but just the prospect of doubt motivated me even more. I dramatically increased my training regimen, hiring a personal trainer who specialized in preparing mountaineers for summit attempts. I signed up for a series of courses, as suggested, and then began progressively attacking more challenging climbs. I went with a team into the Cascade Mountains in Washington State, mostly to practice survival skills and to get used to functioning at high altitude. This was also the first time I was required to wear plastic mountaineering boots—big, heavy, sturdy footwear that provided the insulation and support I needed. After the first day, I counted twelve blisters on my left foot and eleven on my right.

Even with the suffering and annoyances from operating in such difficult conditions, I was feeling really proud of my new skill set. I was getting good at tying knots, I was feeling strong on the climbs, and I found that I had little trouble keeping up with the other team members—most of them men who were much, much bigger and stronger than I am. After completing the weeklong program, I again called Alpine Climbing; by now, the staff knew my story, and we were on a first-name basis. I told them I finished the course. "So, *now* what's next? When do I get to climb Everest?"

"Hold on, there!" I was told. "You've still got a long way to go."

Adventures in the Andes

Sara
July 2013

I'd been making steady progress during the previous months, tackling more progressively difficult peaks in the western United States—mostly in the Cascades in Washington—to practice ice and glacier techniques. One skill that was absolutely critical to master was the "self-arrest" using an ice axe. I first looked at the damn thing and couldn't figure how it was all that useful; in fact, it seemed quite dangerous. There were sharp points on both sides, not to mention the additional twenty-four knife-like points on the crampons attached to my boots. I couldn't imagine tumbling off the side of a mountain without seriously impaling myself on these lethal objects.

To make matters far worse, I learned that I would be roped to three other climbers at all times, usually guys twice my weight. We were supposed to practice "saving" one another in an emergency situation in which one of us fell into a crevasse or slipped off a ridge. I would dutifully dig my crampon spikes into the ice and anchor my ice axe with all my strength, and I could still feel my arms being ripped out of my shoulders. I definitely needed to gain some weight and add more muscle.

None of this training or my practice climbs were even close to the kinds of challenges I would face in the Himalayas, where a single mistake could be fatal. I needed to find some places where I could test myself at higher altitudes, and that meant heading south toward the Andes.

The guides had recommended that an excellent way for me to increase my confidence and proficiency would be to try the huge 6,000-meter volcanoes in Ecuador. All along the Pan-American Highway that crosses the country, picture-perfect snowcapped peaks rise up through the clouds. Since Ecuador is so named because it straddles the equator, it is possible to climb really high mountains in relatively mild weather. And after my freezing night spent on top of Whitney, I still felt an aversion to the cold, one I would eventually have to overcome.

I had mapped out the three main volcanoes I would climb, beginning with Antisana (18,000 feet) and Cotopaxi (19,000 feet) before moving on to Chimborazo, which is the biggest of them all at 20,000 feet. All my ambition and excitement was immediately tempered when I first landed in Quito (9,300 feet): I already had a headache and symptoms of altitude sickness.

I'm not sure what I was thinking when I considered the possibility of breaking my altitude record three times in seventeen days by climbing each of these volcanoes with only a day or two of rest between each expedition. Although the mountains are not especially frigid (by Himalayan standards), the high winds, freezing rain, and constant snow can make the experience fairly miserable, as I was soon to learn. It probably didn't help that I had decided to share my plans to climb Everest with my team and guide, who were, let us say, less than enthusiastic.

"Are you fucking *loca*, Sarita?" my guide asked as he shook his head in bewilderment. He just looked at me and assumed a small woman couldn't possibly be strong enough to attempt something that he could never do.

Once the guide started in on me, it was open season among the other members of my climbing team. "Do you have some kind of death wish?" another woman kept asking me. One guy, perhaps also threatened by the possibility that I could do things beyond his capability, also kept badgering me every time I faltered. "See," he'd say trying to shame me, "how can you possibly *think* about doing Everest?" To be fair, however, there were also a few others on the team who quietly tried to encourage and support me, one of whom was a guy close to eighty years old who had run more than a hundred marathons.

I tried my best just to ignore them, but the criticisms were taking their toll on my (naïve?) confidence.

Too Humiliating to Quit

The idea behind the structured itinerary was to climb progressively higher mountains, resting and recovering in between each expedition. The final climb up Chimborazo would be brutal, not only because we'd be walking all night with no sleep but also because of the rarified air and hurricane-like winds.

The first climb had the easiest approach imaginable: I took a gondola from the middle of Quito up to the top of a 12,000-foot volcano as my starting point. I was in full gear with my pack, helmet, heavy mountaineering boots, and all my equipment, which was kind of amusing since I'd seen all kinds of Ecuadorian families up there enjoying picnics and strolling around like it's a park (which it is). Here I was, tromping around in my boots with trekking poles, and I saw ladies strolling in heels or sandals, carrying their purses instead of backpacks.

The good news was that I ended up making the summit at 15,400 feet without much difficulty. I was really stoked because I'd never been that high before. My headache and slight nausea were totally manageable, and I was feeling pretty strong.

Next on the menu was this gorgeous mountain called Antisana, which has a saddle on top leading to two different summits. The scenery was like a dream, with a glacial lake below us, wild horses running through the pastures, and views of the whole Quito Valley. To add to the excitement, our team consisted of the only people anywhere around.

My optimism took a hit when a substitute guide showed up to lead us; this one who appeared to be somewhat complacent and less than highly motivated. He kept saying, "Take it easy," "*tranquilo*," and "*despacio*." "Take it slowly." That's fine, but what we all needed was a push, not permission to chill out.

For any big climb, the strategy is usually to leave some time before midnight, when the glacier is frozen solid and avalanches would be minimal. During the day, once the sun heats up the ice and snow, the danger increases exponentially—plus there is the added grind of moving in slushy, heavy snow in which you sink to your knees or mid-thighs with every step. The plan is to reach the summit before first light, enjoy the view for a few minutes as the sun rises, and then hurry down (which takes only a few hours) before the mountain becomes unstable.

For reasons I didn't understand, our guide kept us at a low altitude for our base camp. That meant we would have to climb more than 5,000 feet during the night. In addition, rather than getting us going at the usual time, we left four hours late. By the time we'd been climbing for just a few hours, I was already feeling sick. I was so tired from lack of sleep that I could barely keep my eyes open; I was just shuffling along on autopilot trying not to vomit and to keep my head from exploding.

I realized that I hadn't fueled myself properly and didn't have enough nutrition in my system. Getting up this high, beyond 17,000 feet, I also didn't consider how hard it would be to catch my breath. My heart was pounding so hard in my chest that it scared me. I was certain I wasn't getting enough oxygen, and that's when all the cramps began. It was obvious to me at this point that I was not nearly prepared and strong enough to climb such a high summit that was still only a baby peak compared to what I had in mind. It seemed that everyone who had been warning and discouraging me had been right, and I was ready to just turn around and call this whole thing off.

That's when the winds started to pick up. It felt like it was going to blow me right off the edge of the mountain. There were times I had to stop, dig in my pole, turn my back to the wind, and just hold on until I could take another step. Once we arrived at a vertical ice wall, we were temporarily sheltered from the wind. That was the good news; the bad news was that now I had to climb the damn thing, and I was already breathing pretty heavily and sweating through my clothes, freezing the condensation to my body. I noticed that, surprisingly, I still wasn't thirsty, which might have been a good thing because my water bottles were now frozen solid.

The night was completely dark. The only illumination possible was from my headlamp as well as those of other team members. I decided that was a gift of sorts, because the one time I decided to peer over the edge of the ridge we were climbing, there was a deep crevasse that didn't seem to end. Better that I just kept my light and eyes right in front of me. I was becoming so terrified of falling that I forgot how hard I was breathing. I started to climb the wall just as fast as I could, hoping to get to safety as soon as possible and enjoy some rest. The few times I stopped to eat, the energy bars were frozen solid. I thought I'd break my teeth.

There was this constant dialogue going on inside my head. I kept negotiating with myself: "In five more minutes, if I don't feel any better, I'll take a break." "If this headache doesn't go away in the next half hour, I'll turn back." And then, being mathematically inclined, I tried to estimate what percentage of energy I thought I might have left. I came up with a rather precise answer of "seven percent," which didn't inspire much confidence. Since I was roped to my partners, before I could change my mind, I would just get pulled along. Given what I'd told the others about my plans, it felt too humiliating to quit.

I Lost My Motivation—and a Part of Myself

Climbing a big mountain is a grind. There's usually nothing to see because it is dark during the ascent. It's just one endless footstep after another, following the snaking headlights ahead: one step, two steps, four steps, breathe, rest. Repeat. Over and over and over again. The only variation was when the slope was too steep to walk forward and I was forced to sidestep, crossing one leg over the other until my hips started to ache.

After four hours of this grueling routine, I could see the first glimmer of the sun about to peak over the far ridge. There was this incredible golden line across the horizon, and for the first time, I could actually see all the spectacular volcanoes and valleys around us. Even though I still had a headache and nausea, I was temporarily distracted enough to realize that this was the most beautiful thing I'd ever seen, (almost) making it worth all the suffering and aggravation.

This joy didn't last more than a minute before I realized what bad shape I was in. I was not only absolutely exhausted; I also felt totally disoriented, barely aware of where I was and what I was doing there. I kept collapsing to the ground, then wondering how I got there. I'd slowly, agonizingly use my trekking pole in one hand and my ice axe in the other to pull myself back to a standing position. Then I'd take another step or two and end up on the ground again. It felt hopeless, and I wondered how I could possibly continue. At this point, I was also wondering how I was going to get back down, no longer concerned with reaching the summit.

Through my fog, I heard one of the other team members announce that he'd had enough and was going back down. Before I could think about whether I wanted to join him or not, the rest of the climbers who were attached to his rope immediately decided to join mine, which I was none too happy about. I had enough problems already without having to deal with another group of climbers who would likely climb at a different rhythm and pace. This one guy in particular kept pulling on my rope to make me go faster, so I just pulled back. Finally, I was so angry and frustrated with him that I screamed, "Goddamn it! Will you stop pulling on the damn rope and leave me alone!" I heard the words coming out of my mouth, but it was as if they belonged to someone else. I no longer recognized myself.

Only later would I realize that I was experiencing the most severe form of altitude symptoms: high-altitude cerebral edema. I knew that *something* was wrong with me, but I wasn't thinking clearly enough to know what was happening. Because of increasing fluid accumulation in my tissue, the symptoms would never dissipate until I headed back down to a much lower altitude. I was especially worried because I'd eaten so little food, had no appetite, and all I could think about was trying to avoid throwing up.

"Just get it over with," one of the guides instructed me. "Just throw up, and you'll feel better."

Easy for him to say. I was barely keeping myself together. I was wondering how I could possibly continue when the lead guide announced we couldn't make the summit that morning because the ice bridge had collapsed. I could hear some token grumbling, but I think all of us were relieved that we could head back down to safety and warmth. And once we descended a few thousand feet rather quickly, I could already feel myself recovering. As dispirited as I felt, I glanced over my shoulder and saw Cotopaxi in the distance, with its symmetrical snowcap glistening in the sun. I knew that was where we were headed in a few more days.

I thought I might feel better after I had a decent meal and caught up on some sleep. That wasn't exactly the case, especially after I felt further discouraged when one of the guides remarked that there were just some people who couldn't handle high altitude. He was implying that I was one of those people.

Round Two

Like a punch-drunk boxer still reeling from too many hits to the head, I wasn't quite myself when we began the ascent of Cotopaxi a few days later. As usual, it was windy and sleeting. Because summit attempts begin around midnight, it is almost impossible to get any sleep between the excitement, high-altitude insomnia, and noisy snoring among those who are oblivious.

Picture yourself trying to sleep in a freezing room with fourteen other people, crammed together and, practically touching one another. The wind is howling so loudly the windows are rattling. While you lie in your sleeping bag, terribly anxious about whether you are going to even survive the night, you hear the guides snoring and people sneezing, coughing, farting, and repositioning themselves. Sleep is impossible, so the hours drag on.

I felt such relief when it was finally time to get started, but once again, I had a vicious headache and no appetite whatsoever. I forced myself to stuff a few bites of a sandwich in my mouth and drank some tepid soup. I looked over at the guides, who were well rested, and watched them devour a huge meal, making me feel even more nauseous.

After just two hours on the mountain, I already looked like a human icicle. I climbed in a stupor all night long, one agonizing step after another. I kept my eyes and my headlamp focused only on my feet and the space ahead of me. Some of the time we were walking on a knife edge of a ridge; a fall would surely mean death, as I couldn't imagine that anything would save me. At times the glacier was so steep that we were practically crawling on our hands and knees. At other times, it was once again just a long, endless, brutal slog, hour after hour. Remarkably, somehow we were finally approaching the summit, which was just fifty meters away—the top was literally within a snowball's throw.

I saw a guy coming down from the top. He was so covered in snow and ice that, at first, he didn't look human at all. His eyelashes and beard were frozen solid. "How was the view?" I called out to him.

"What view?" he answered through the howling wind. "It's like being in a hurricane up there. It's hard to even stay upright without getting blown off."

That's all I needed to hear. What was the point of getting to the top if the only reason is to say you did it? There was no view, no enjoyment of the moment—just bitter, bitter cold that drives you into the ground.

My legs felt rubbery and insubstantial. Most people think that getting to the summit is the hardest part about a climb, and I suppose it is, in the sense that it is the most physically demanding part. But it's usually on the way down that most people get injured or die because of their exhaustion and sense of urgency. You aren't thinking straight. You are likely descending too fast.

Once again, I kept falling until, at one point, disaster occurred: I fell right into a deep crevasse. I found myself hanging from a rope as I heard people screaming, but strangely, I wasn't scared. On the contrary; I was fascinated by the eerie deep-turquoise color of the cave with huge icicles hanging down from every surface. It was so beautiful, I thought for a moment that I had died.

Then I felt myself being hauled out of the hole. Everyone on the team was working in unison, absolutely freaked out by my close call. As I mentioned before, we were roped together for safety in case one of us took a fall. The moment you lose control, you are supposed to scream, "Falling!" so everyone immediately gets into the proper position for a rescue. We practice this over and over, so it is second nature; in an emergency situation, there is no time to think, only to react.

This time I was lucky, because I was the lightest person on the rope, and it was easy for them to hold on to me and keep me from slipping further into nothingness. I could hear everyone freaking out above me, but I felt totally calm, almost mesmerized by the view down inside this bluish glacier. I was so tired of walking anyway that I just wanted to hang from the rope and rest as long as possible. I was actually disappointed that my team pulled me out before I was ready.

Once I popped out of the hole, I could see that not everyone was happy with the situation. Our guide was furious at me because I forgot to yell "Falling!" as I sailed off the edge. There were a few other things I considered yelling as I lost my balance, but "Falling!" wasn't one of them. I was certainly grateful for the rescue, though, so that I might live and climb another day.

Round Three ... Postponed

It took me three days to mostly recover from the previous failed climb, and there was still one more to go: the highest of them all, Chimborazo. This volcano is actually 7,000 feet higher than the top of Everest—at least if you measure from the center of the earth.

At the last minute, I decided to cancel my final climb and rest at the hut at 16,000 feet until the rest of the group returned, but because of the bad weather, the whole climb was cancelled anyway. We went back to Quito for a couple of days before heading back home.

At this point, life intervened. I was feeling increasingly fearful about risking my life. I was tired of feeling like a failure, that I couldn't handle these challenges.

So when I was offered two teaching positions, I accepted; it was a dream I'd never thought to pursue. I was feeling discouraged by my climbing efforts, and when this opportunity arose, I couldn't pass it up.

When I was a kid, I would arrange all my dolls on the bed like a classroom, tape a sheet of paper on the wall, and teach them math. I'd drill them in their addition and subtraction numbers. I didn't think that girls could ever become professors, especially since we were barely allowed to pursue an education at all.

And after working a few years as an electrical engineer on different projects, sitting in front of a computer screen all day studying and modifying electrical circuits, I desperately needed new challenges.

Even though the pay was less than half of what I'd received at my engineering job, I was much happier and more satisfied. Seeing the spark in students' eyes that came from learning new material and being empowered to use it at their jobs was priceless. I could see myself doing this for the rest of my life. I also started getting comfortable talking in front of people, which was shocking to me. My leadership seminars were definitely helping to improve my confidence and speaking ability.

I was soon fully immersed in my new career as an electrical engineering and computer science professor, teaching at two different universities. This meant that as a new hire, I had to accept almost any class offered, regardless of the specific subject and the time it was offered. I no longer had time for my training, so I put my climbing career on hold while I tried to establish myself as an academic and get used to the idea I was now actually a real-life professor, another goal that I could never have imagined was possible.

While I was completing my first semester teaching, my friend Pari suggested that I make contact with the professor she'd often mentioned. Jeffrey Kottler, who also taught psychotherapists at the university where I was now employed, also enjoyed climbing mountains and was doing a lot of work in Nepal. I immediately sent him a message, asking if we could meet so I could learn more about the things he was doing. It just seemed like a strange coincidence that this guy was spending so much time in the area I yearned to go to.

As soon as I entered his office, Jeffrey gave me the warmest, most inviting smile, as if we were already old friends. "So," he started the conversation, "what do you teach here? I haven't seen you before."

"That's because this is my first semester," I explained, still feeling a bit shy. My friends had told me that Dr. Kottler had written more books than most people had ever read, and he was an international scholar. "Anyway, I teach courses in data structure and microelectronics."

"I have no idea what those are," he said with a grin, "but I'm glad somebody knows how to teach those things."

I asked him about Nepal and his experiences there, but rather than talking about his travels in the Himalayas, he talked instead about the plight of girls there. He told me the story of how he got started there many years ago when he was working on a research project and the ways that women and girls were treated in that country, sometimes forced into slavery.

Jeffrey said that fifteen years earler he had been doing research with a doctoral student, a Nepali obstetrician and public health official who was doing a study to investigate the high rate of maternal mortality. More women die in childbirth in Nepal than almost anywhere else in the world. This isn't that surprising, considering that 90 percent of the people had no access to healthcare whatsoever, but even more perplexing to this physician was that even when there was a health professional in the region, the women would not seek their services. Jeffrey and his doctoral student were trying to figure out why.

It turns out that during their interviews with new mothers, they learned that the women felt humiliated and shamed when they visited a hospital or clinic. The doctors were almost all men, and they treated these lower-caste women like animals. The women would return to their villages and announce that it was better to die rather than subject themselves to having men touch their private parts and put "snakes in their arms." The doctors would insert intravenous tubes but never explain what they were for or why they were necessary.

It was while visiting these remote villages that Jeffrey first learned that girls were "disappearing." This was a rather unusual way to describe children who were missing, and Jeffrey couldn't figure out what this really meant—that is, until a school principal pointed to one twelve-year-old girl and mentioned that she would be "disappeared" next. Apparently, her father was an alcoholic and had abandoned the family, leaving them destitute.

When Jeffrey asked the principal what happens to the girls, the principal explained that they end up going to work in India. When pressed further, the principal reluctantly explained that this "job" actually involved becoming a sex slave in one of the brothels in Mumbai. There is a belief among some Indian men who are HIV positive that if they have sex with a virgin, it will cure their disease.

This was just about the most horrifying thing he had ever heard. Nine- and ten-year-old girls being sold as sex slaves? Jeffrey mentioned that more than ten thousand girls each year are abducted or sold into sex slavery in Nepal, some as young as seven years old. But what really knocked Jeffrey for a loop wasn't these statistics but the principal pointing to that twelve-year-old girl standing in the schoolyard and informing him that she would be disappeared next.

Jeffrey impulsively reached into his pocket to give the principal money to keep this girl safe and out of harm's way. He believed, in that moment, that this was the single most significant thing he'd ever done in his life—saving a girl's life for the cost of a good meal. He told me he started sobbing because he was so moved and grateful for this opportunity—that is, until his doctoral student informed him that the principal would likely just keep the money. Unless Jeffrey was prepared to return to this village and check on the girl, her fate was already sealed.

"So, that's how it all started," Jeffrey explained. Since then his charity had grown exponentially expanding all over the country and involving volunteers from all over the world. There were now hundreds of girls, in more than a dozen villages, who were being supported and mentored in this program. Some of the first scholarship girls were now attending higher education, the first in their villages to ever do so.

Even more interesting to me was that Jeffrey led groups of volunteers each year to Nepal, all of whom raised money to support the girls and mentor their education. The team members would travel around the country conducting home visits, volunteering in the schools, awarding scholarships, and then reporting back to donors exactly how their money was being spent. Then, he suprisied me when he suddenly asked me if I might like to join them during their next visit and perhaps combine it with a climbing expedition.

Everything I knew about Nepal was related to summiting Everest. I had been single-minded in my focus. I had yet to consider what life was like in the country for the people who live in these remote areas. Jeffrey explained how difficult and challenging life was for girls from the lowest caste who had so few opportunities. So many lived in poverty and neglect, and so vulnerable to exploitation.

As I sat in Jeffrey's office listening to this story, *everything* changed for me in that moment. I realized that one reason I might have been having such difficulty with the physical challenges of my previous climbs was that it never made sense to me to climb a mountain just for the personal glory. The sacrifices, discomforts, and misery zapped my resolve because my goal was so self-centered, and all along, I had been searching for some greater meaning and purpose. I wondered what it would feel like to risk my life, not for a trophy or personal achievement but for some greater good.

Until this point, I was trying to prove to my family and friends—and my father—that I'm strong. My culture had so limited me. I was angry about how often I was underestimated. I thought about what it must be like for these girls in Nepal who, like me, had so few opportunities and options. I wondered how I might inspire them, not just by raising money but through my actions on the mountain.

Jeffrey shared his story with me: how his impulsivity led to trying to save one girl and how that had grown into a movement and then an organization supporting hundreds. I found his enthusiasm and passion contagious, so much so that I blurted out my own commitment.

"How about this?" I said to him, the words rushing out before I could even think things through. "I'd *love* to meet the girls and have some reason to climb Everest other than just to get to the top. What if I could show them what a woman who looks like them, who also comes from a similar background, can do if she puts her mind to it?"

"Sure, sounds good," he replied, "but—"

"Wait!" I interrupted with building excitement. "I have this idea. I think I can raise a lot of money for the girls. In fact, Everest is 29,000 feet."

"Yeah?" Jeffrey said, confused about where this was going.

"I will raise one dollar for every foot of Everest that I climb. That's $29,000!"

"Okay," he answered. "That would be the biggest donation we've ever had. That would be awesome if you could raise even a small part of that. Just as important is for the children to meet you and see you as someone they might become—an educated, powerful professional woman who can not only climb the highest mountains in the world but also support your family."

As I left Jeffrey's office, I was more determined than ever to climb Everest, but now I would do it to plant the flag of Empower Nepali Girls—the organization he was involved with—on the highest spot in the world. There had to be some way I could continue my teaching responsibilities yet also renew my commitment to training harder than ever before. I felt a new sense of purpose. Given where I came from and what I had to live through as a girl in Iran, I felt a deep connection to these girls I would soon meet in person. I recognized a part of myself in every one of them.

I Followed Sara's Footsteps

Jeffrey
September 2013

"Who *was* that woman?" I asked myself after Sara left my office following that first meeting. "Where has she been hiding herself?" I wondered. For so many years, I'd been searching far and wide for powerful, inspirational women who could help us with the foundation in Nepal. My wife, Ellen, and many of my graduate students had been volunteering part-time—assisting with bookkeeping, fundraising, marketing, and other functions—but we desperately needed someone in a more visible leadership role.

On some level, I'd always felt uncomfortable as an older white male being in charge of an organization devoted to helping young marginalized girls. Then Sara showed up, and it became obvious that her passion, enthusiasm, and interest in our work was a perfect match.

I know she was intrigued by the stories I told her about the girls in Nepal. I'd only just met her, but I could tell right away that there was some deep connection she felt toward what we were doing. She seemed so excited about the idea that her visits to Nepal would become something more than just climbing Everest to accomplish some personal goal. I noticed how excited she became when she talked about how she might bring greater attention to the plight of girl trafficking. But what surprised me just as much was how entranced I became by Sara's story and her climbing adventures. Although I had been to Nepal dozens of times and completed almost every one of the major treks over the years, I had never scaled a major summit. The clock was ticking now that I was in my mid-sixties, so I knew there wasn't much time left if I ever wanted to accomplish that goal.

When Sara walked out of my office, she thanked me profusely, as if I had offered her some kind of gift. And there was little doubt that something came together for her in a profound way. But I was also reeling from an idea she'd planted in my head. After hearing about some of Sara's adventures, I found myself yearning to create some more of my own. It sounded like she was having so much fun and learning so much about herself that I wanted some of the action as well.

The main challenge in trying to keep up with Sara, or at least follow in her footsteps, was the thirty-year difference in our ages. Lately I'd been struggling with adjusting to the symptoms of aging and found that things that I used to be able to do were now so much more difficult. I had always thought that aging was a relatively gradual, incremental process that proceeded in an orderly fashion from one stage to the next. I've taught courses in human development over the years, so I'm more than a little familiar with all the research on the subject. So I was quite dumbfounded to discover that within a ridiculously short period of time, I had become old. My body was indeed slowing down, and my mind was not what it used to be.

Sara had made it sound so easy and fun to travel down to Ecuador. She told me the scenery was absolutely spectacular, the volcanoes gorgeous beyond imagination, and the social scene in Quito unparalleled. She raved about the food (ceviche, potato soup) and how friendly the locals were. She said that with all my experience in Nepal, it would be no problem for me to do some of the climbs there.

I started training for the expedition with ferocious commitment, increasing my workout regimens several hours each day. I invested in mountaineering equipment and trained to become comfortable with my boots, crampons, and other gear. I spent hours on a stair climber with a bag full of books on my back. I planned my acclimatization to high altitude with careful and meticulous incremental adjustments. After all, I wasn't a young man anymore, and I wanted to survive this experience more than I needed to summit the volcanoes.

Things did not go quite according to my plan. My guide, Enrico, turned out to be more interested in getting me to the top than being worried about my safety. He seemed to take pleasure in shaming and cajoling me to go faster and harder. At my age, I have to pee a lot, and I was incensed that he wouldn't even allow me to stop occasionally to relieve myself. He said it would take too long to remove my climbing harness and all my equipment, so I was instructed to just hold it.

We had begun the summit of Cotopaxi at 10:00 p.m., having had to start several hours earlier than usual because of closed facilities at the preferred staging point, which was at a higher altitude. As we climbed up, up, up, I tried to get into a rhythm that felt comfortable, a task that was becoming increasingly challenging as we ascended higher. I could feel Enrico pulling me on the rope, urging me to go faster. I wasn't sure why it was so important that we move so quickly instead of at my own pace, but maybe it was because we had to start so much further down the mountain and needed to make up time before the snow softened when the sun came up.

It was completely dark, our trail lit by headlamps directed only at the next few steps ahead. Sara had told me that the glacier was speckled with deep crevasses, but I was still surprised when I looked to the left or right and saw we were walking on the knife edge of a ridge with a drop-off of thousands of feet on each side. I kept trying to rehearse in my mind what to do if I slipped. For some strange reason, all I could think of was that it was important to yell, "Falling!" like Sara had forgotten to do when she slipped into the crevasse. I was tired of Enrico yelling at me. Oh, did I mention I'm afraid of heights?

My breathing was becoming ragged, and I started feeling light-headed as we topped over 17,000 feet. It had been a long, long night so far, climbing for five hours. And just like Sara's climb, it was the usual weather on Cotopaxi— rain, sleet, snow, and fifty-mile-an-hour winds. I kept asking myself every few minutes, "*Why* did I think this was a good idea?"

It was about three o'clock in the morning, still hours from the summit, when I kept hearing this voice inside my head becoming more and more strident. *You know, you don't have to do this. You can stop any time you want.* It felt like I was hallucinating because the voice seemed to come from someone else. I looked ahead at Enrico trudging along at his own comfortable pace and wondered for a moment whether he was the one speaking to me. But he ignored me most of the time. I was just a burden to him, a package to deliver to the top.

I could barely catch my breath anymore. I'd take two steps then need to rest for a moment, leaning on my ice axe before I could feel Enrico yanking my rope once again. "*Nos vamos!* Let's go!" he'd say with an infuriating smile, almost seeming to enjoy my discomfort and difficulty. This time when he pulled on my rope, I yanked it back as hard as I could, almost pulling him over. I could hear him swearing at me, and I stifled a giggle of satisfaction.

At that moment, I realized I was in *way* over my ability. I was too old, or at least too old to climb at someone else's pace—someone who was much younger than me (and a professional mountaineer). I had to respect my limits—and my age. So I unhooked the rope from my waist, turned off my headlamp, and lay down on the glacier, staring up at the moon.

I stripped off my pack, stuck my axe into the ice, and just lay down on the glacier. The skies had temporarily cleared for a few minutes before the next blizzard would begin, so I could see the whole universe above me. I could hear the sounds of the glacier groaning as it settled and resettled itself—an animal-like sound, as if it was truly alive. I could almost feel it pulsing underneath me.

I lay there for I don't know how long. It could have been ten minutes or a half hour, I'm not sure. I tried to just ignore Enrico, who was sitting off by himself eating a snack and humming to himself. At least he was leaving me alone for a change.

In some ways, those few peaceful minutes on the glacier, just lying there and listening to the glacial movements, made the whole trip worthwhile. During this interlude, there was no suffering or discomfort, just complete and utter peace. I never wanted the experience to end—except that I was now getting quite cold, and it was time to begin the descent.

Enrico didn't seem to care if we stayed there or not, but I could see he was becoming increasingly restless to keep going. All I wanted to do was get down the mountain and feel warm again. I was surrendering to the realities of my age. It was time to accept my limitations and make do with what was still within my capability. I learned a hard lesson, but perhaps one that would serve me well during this next stage of life.

Beyond Myself

When I returned from Ecuador, in some ways I was actually proud of my decision to *not* reach the summit. I thought this was quite an excellent example of wise, mature decision-making. I told Sara about my misfortune on Cotopaxi, and she confessed to me that she hadn't made it to the summit either! It's not that she had been hiding anything from me; I just didn't think to ask her much about the climb itself other than what equipment I'd need.

But once I learned that Sara hadn't made it to the top, it felt like I still had unfinished business on that mountain. I figured if I prepared differently, trained harder, and, especially, worked with a different guide, I could conquer that sucker after all. I also planned to bring my wife, Ellen, with me for moral support.

When I contacted the mountaineering company in Ecuador, they promised me I could have a different guide and even offered me a repeat customer discount. I was waiting for my pickup outside the *hosteria* where I was staying when who shows up but Enrico! *This is impossible*, I thought; I'd specially requested *any* other guide except him.

I was still optimistic about my chances of summiting because I knew that the upper lodge was now open, so we could begin the climb a few hours earlier and a few thousand feet higher than last time, which would definitely help. Unfortunately, Enrico explained we'd be staying at the same place as last time because he'd forgotten to make a reservation at the high camp. Foiled again!

This time, we began the climb at 9:00 p.m.—three hours earlier than should have been necessary—but I was feeling particularly strong. I had made sure to fuel up as much as I could, forcing food down my throat. I'd still not gotten any sleep during our rest time, but I could feel my adrenaline flowing in anticipation.

By the time we reached the high camp where everyone else was staying, it was close to midnight, and they were all gearing up, seemingly well rested and well fed. Me? I was already tired.

Things went spectacularly well during the night. It was remarkably clear. In all the time I'd spent in Ecuador during these trips, I'd never actually had a clear night without a cloud in the sky. The only ominous news was that Cotopaxi, as an active volcano, was due for a major eruption. There were billows of smoke flowing from the top.

Besides Enrico and me, at least a half dozen other teams were heading for the summit, with only one very narrow trail of switchbacks across and over the glacier. We kept trying to pass the teams ahead of us. As I mentioned, Enrico was a fast walker, but this time I was keeping up with him. He also must have been in a better mood this time, because he seemed unusually gracious and patient with me.

Of course, a few hours later, the freezing rain and sleet started to come down, blowing horizontally with the strong winds. Once we reached over 18,000 feet, things got even worse, with absolutely no visibility.

We were only a few hundred meters from the summit, and I felt completely depleted. In addition, we were now in the middle of a raging blizzard, compounded by all the smoke seeping out of the volcano. I could see other climbers heading down from the top, and they looked grim and miserable "What's up there?" I yelled as they passed by. "Anything to see up there?" One guy just shook his head; the others ignored me.

I knew I'd come all the way back here specifically to conquer this infernal mountain, but now I reconsidered once again what the point was. I don't do this sort of thing to notch some triumph on my belt but rather to enjoy the journey and adventure of it all. I tell patients and students all the time that it isn't just their goals that are important but also the process of getting there. In many ways, it is the experience that is far more important that the achievement.

"Enrico," I said in a tired voice. "I think I've had enough. There's nothing to see up there. I don't see the point of going further just to say I've been there. Let's take our time going back down and enjoy the views."

Miraculously, the weather started to clear just about the time we started down. The darkening sky of nighttime was actually turning fluorescent blue. I could see the sun peeking above the horizon, lighting up the volcanic peaks all around us. There were incredible ice sculptures everywhere, carved by winds and glaciers. Even though my legs were rubbery, my back was killing me, I hadn't slept in over thirty hours, and I was starving, dehydrated, and exhausted, I felt giddy, almost dancing with glee as we made our way down the trail. *This* is what I came for—not to get to the summit, not to test the limits of my aging, but to earn the right to see this gorgeous sunrise over the Andes.

I thought about Sara's own experience on these volcanoes: how initially she had failed to summit but learned to adapt and find new sources of motivation. Sara's passion and exuberance had inspired me to go beyond what I imagined was possible. Just as I found myself following in her footsteps in the mountains, I started to imagine what she could do for the girls in Nepal. These were children who rarely, if ever, encountered a woman—especially someone who looked like them—who was educated as an engineer and tried to conquer mountains.

From all my experience and work in Nepal during the previous decade, I had had so many disappointments and betrayals. There was so much corruption and fraud. There were so many different ethnic, caste, and tribal groups that it seemed fruitless at times to unite them for a common cause. The country hadn't had a stable government in years, and this would continue through a civil war, assassination of their king, endless elections, strikes, and political upheaval. It wasn't enough for me to raise money and recruit more volunteers; more than anything, we needed someone who could actually show girls, their families, and the village leaders that a strong, powerful, educated women could do *anything*. And Sara was that woman.

6

A New Plan

Sara
December 2013

My mind was racing with ideas and possibilities for raising money to support my Everest fundraising idea. It occurred to me that when I was having moments of doubt during climbs, when I felt exhausted and wanted to give up, the girls would inspire me to keep going—not for myself, but for them. Now my climbing goals were only partially related to successful summits—far more important was the attention I could bring to this important cause: protecting the safety of children. I had yet to meet the girls, but I was already imagining myself talking to them about how strong and resourceful young women can be if they're given a chance. If things in Nepal were anything like back home in Iran, I didn't think they'd had many opportunities to see women in positions of power.

Of course, I'd never tried fundraising before, but that didn't stop me: I'd also never been climbing before I decided to scale Everest. The Persian community in Southern California is very tight-knit and quite generous in helping less fortunate people. Although I did get some questions from some within the community as to why I wasn't helping Persian girls instead of Hindu/Buddhist children in a country they'd barely heard of, I explained that it didn't matter who we were helping as long as we were doing *something* to make the world a better place.

I tried all kinds of things to get started: organizing dinner parties, silent auctions, lectures, and charity events as well as using social media to publicize my plans and ask for support. I was shocked not only by how many friends and family joined my effort but also that I had a talent for this kind of thing.

I had watched Jeffrey do a few presentations to large groups, and I noticed that his main goal was to move the audience emotionally. He would begin with a few stories about the girls and their struggles, then talk about how a little effort or minimal contributions could make such a huge difference in their lives. He also talked about how, as an organization, they had completely reconceptualized how a charity could operate, keeping overhead to an absolute minimum and relying on volunteers exclusively so that all of the donations could go directly to support the children's education.

Since one of my future goals involved becoming more involved in leadership, I made it a priority to train as a public speaker in much the same way I was devoted to mountaineering. I started studying TED Talks and, given my propensity to declare ridiculously unrealistic goals, decided that someday I would be invited to do one myself (and eventualy I was!). Meanwhile, I needed to work on my confidence. It was one thing to present a class lecture on capacitors, transistors, regulators, and transformers in engineering and quite another to inspire and motivate an audience to get on board with our mission.

I hated asking people for money. I hated even asking my mother for money to buy food when I was hungry at school. Now I had to beg perfect strangers for money even though I had no experience in sales or marketing. Predictably I made a lot of mistakes, not unlike my experiences as a neophyte mountaineer.

At most of my early events, very few people showed up or expressed much interest in what I was doing. Yet climbing had taught me how to fight this discouragement and remain motivated even though I was not very effective in reaching my goal. When climbing a big mountain, we don't try for the summit in one shot. We are constantly going up, and then down, in order to acclimatize. After all the effort and work it takes to make it up to a high camp, we head back down to recover and start over again. And again. Each time, making more progress. It seemed to be an important lesson for my current enterprise: expecting initial disappointments until things came together.

Even though I was still a neophyte at public speaking, I loved that I could measure my success by the amount of money flowing in to support the girls. Within just a few months, I'd already raised so much money that I decided to increase my initial audacious target. Jeffrey told me that I was now the most successful fundraiser they'd ever had. As wonderful as that felt, I still had to concentrate on getting back into training if I was serious about my commitment to climb Everest.

Heading South

I reintroduced myself to the people at Alpine Climbing, who hadn't heard from me in a while and must have assumed I had disappeared. "It's me again," I told the guide on the phone, "you know, the lady who wants to climb Everest but hadn't had any mountaineering experience."

"Yes?" the guide said, seemingly distracted, or perhaps confused. I don't really think he had any idea who I was, so I reviewed for him what I'd been told earlier. "I took the advice you guys gave me and tried climbing Whitney, then Rainier, then I went to Ecuador and did the volcanoes there as you told me to do."

"Yeah? How did it go?"

"Fine," I lied. "So tell me. What's next?"

The guide explained that now that I'd completed all those preliminary training climbs, I needed to demonstrate that I could handle a 7,000-meter peak before I could join one of their expeditions.

"Okay, then where should I go?"

"You say you've done Ecuador?"

I'm not sure what he meant by "done," but I had certainly spent time on some of those volcanoes.

"The next mountain you should try, then, is Aconcagua," he answered after only a moment's thought.

"Oh yeah? Where's that?" I asked.

"It's in Argentina, near the Chilean border. It's the highest mountain in the Western Hemisphere—over 23,000 feet high. Let us know when you've done that, and then we can talk about you joining one of our qualifying expeditions in the Himalayas."

This wasn't going to be like Ecuador at all, where I could go up and down in two days. This climb was going to take close to a month, with twenty days spent continuously on the glacier. I planned to do a few things differently, starting with upping my training regimen. I also decided I wasn't going to tell anyone on the trip about my Everest plans, because I was tired of people making fun of me. Best to just keep that to myself.

High in the Andes

Once I arrived in Mendoza, Argentina, I met our team and was immediately reassured, since everyone was about my age and had not much experience climbing. Two of the guys were from the United Arab Emirates. They were tall, muscular, and obviously privileged, by the look of their high-end equipment. I was on a strict budget, renting plastic mountaineering boots that hurt my feet, so I was envious. I was quickly introduced to Katrina, an older woman about my mom's age, who would be my tentmate. I was immediately impressed by her because she managed to juggle family responsibilities with a career as a business executive, yet she still found time to pursue climbing.

Once we started the climb, Katrina was struck by bad altitude sickness, with all the worst symptoms—nausea, insomnia, vertigo, fatigue, loss of appetite, vomiting, and headaches. I felt responsible for her and decided it was my job to take care of her. In some ways, being so worried about her health and safety helped to distract me from my own discomforts and challenges. This also meant that I had to assume more of the daily tasks—setting up our tent and organizing our gear—since much of the time, Katrina was pretty much out of it.

I had already been exposed to high winds on the Ecuadorian volcanoes, but I wasn't prepared for the hurricane force I encountered on Aconcagua. It wasn't supposed to be that technical of a climb, but when you are trying to sleep in a tent at high altitude with sixty-mile-per-hour winds threatening to blow you off the mountain, you have no choice but to slip back into survival mode, just like I had on that lonely night on Whitney. This time, however, at least I wasn't alone in my misery, since Katrina was suffering far worse.

We had to spend two nights and three days trapped in our tents because it wasn't safe to venture outside. This was also the first time I learned the "funnel technique" for peeing in a bottle, an absolute necessity for women who don't have the luxury of simply inserting an organ into the opening. All I could do during that time was try to stay as warm as possible in my sleeping bag and stare at the mesh ceiling of the tent, since sleep was out of the question. Katrina and I did try at times to talk about our lives and dreams, but most of the time we just kept to our own miserable thoughts.

When the high winds finally diminished to only "raging," we geared up and began climbing again, this time to Camp IV at 21,000 feet, the highest point I'd ever reached. This would be our final staging area for the summit attempt after spending a few more days acclimatizing to the rarified air. Given that sleep was out of the question at such altitude, it wasn't exactly restful, hanging out waiting for the weather to clear. Everything is challenging at that altitude: it takes forever just to boil water and prepare a meal. And one of the biggest challenges is consuming enough calories to maintain strength after so many days on the mountain. We were all getting anxious and excited for the final stage.

There was a mystery in our little camp that a few of us were trying to solve. We noticed a solitary abandoned tent on the edge of our ridge, one of the few reasonably flat spaces before the mountain rose in a steep vertical wall. The tent was mostly tattered by the high winds, but when we investigated, we noticed there was some valuable gear inside. When we asked one of the guides why the tent was there and who it belonged to, he just shrugged and pointed to the summit. Apparently, two climbers had left for the summit a few days earlier and were now trapped somewhere on the way up. We could see a helicopter flying over us, presumably to try and rescue them, but we later learned their bodies were never found.

As if that wasn't enough of a bad omen, there was another tent in the vicinity with two climbers who were so sick they couldn't move. Our guides intervened to pack them up and send them back down so they might survive before they became worse. Watching these two incidents made us all even more concerned about our safety.

There is a problem for climbers: at high altitude, you burn something like five thousand calories per day, and it's virtually impossible to replace all that lost energy. In addition, you usually have no appetite in general, which is compounded by the tasteless freeze-dried food and energy bars. Our guides kept reminding us to eat and drink as much as we could, even though it was just one more chore we had to get done.

I craved variety in my diet, especially meat and sweets, but those were somewhat rare in my home growing up. Yet I never figured how much worse things could be when you are limited to dehydrated rice and beans, dehydrated scrambled eggs, and energy bars that are frozen solid. It was the same menu every day. With every bite, I kept repeating a mantra to myself: "Don't throw up. Don't throw up." I also resented that the guides controlled every aspect of my daily existence: when I woke up or went to sleep, what I was permitted to do and what was forbidden, and what I was allowed to consume, in whatever quantities they determined.

One of my guides was fond of quoting famous writers who reflected on mountaineering, and I remembered one in particular that stuck in my mind as I'd stare at a bowl of tasteless, watery oatmeal. I think it was from Mark Twain, and it went something like this: "There is probably no pleasure equal to the pleasure of climbing a dangerous mountain, but it is a pleasure that is limited strictly to people who can find pleasure in such a thing." Well, it had been at least a week since I could remember finding much pleasure in what we were doing.

If consuming enough food and water was one difficulty, then another was dealing with things on the other end, so to speak. Constipation was killing me as we kept going higher and higher. In order to have a bowel movement, I had to either use the vestibule of my tent where the flap folds over (which is fairly disgusting) or wander out on the glacier in the freezing wind—in full view of everyone else, since there was nothing to hide behind. I had never considered how hard it was to do anything up here and how many of my prior "rules" as a modest Persian woman I would have to break.

Cold Fingers

The days wore on, with very little change in routines. It was like we were hibernating, waiting for a break in the weather in order to crawl out of our den. During this isolated time, I began keeping a journal to describe my innermost private thoughts and feelings. I was writing in Farsi, my native language, and that allowed me to express some of my deepest fears and doubts. I had no paper with me, and there wasn't exactly an opportunity to acquire any on top of the world, so I resorted to writing in the margins of a book I'd been reading. I think this was the beginning of my discovery that I might have something meaningful to say.

When Katrina was passed out or I was just restless with boredom, I'd take a "bath" with wet wipes, scrubbing sections of my body with the alcohol-infused pads. And then there was the constant organizing and reorganizing of my equipment, which I could never seem to find when I needed it most. Where was my spare camera battery, or the heat warmers for my gloves, or the treat I'd been saving? I frequently seemed to have misplaced certain things, which would drive me crazy because they were tucked away in some pocket or compartment.

Finally, after days and days of claustrophobic isolation, it was summit night! We tried to grab a few hours of sleep, which was futile, and then we emerged from our cocoons into the frigid cold. I'm talking about the kind of cold that is so brutal that any exposed flesh will turn black in minutes. Twenty degrees below zero. Sixty-mile-an-hour winds. It hurt to take a deep breath.

I looked outside my tent and saw one of our guides, Mariano, just standing there, looking out at the horizon. I was shivering so much already that I was trying to muster the courage to step outside, yet he was casually sipping coffee and watching the sunset.

"What are you doing out there?" I screamed above the howling wind, not at all certain he could even hear me.

He seemed to shrug, or at least his shoulders moved.

"Aren't you cold standing out there?" I yelled again.

Mariano turned to look at me. "I guess you get used to it." He paused for a moment, then added, "That's why I'm here. This is my life, so I better enjoy it."

Fortunately, once we started climbing, I immediately felt warm. And strong! As we ascended slowly, steadily, it felt like my hands were burning up. I didn't realize at the time that this is one of the crazy effects of high altitude. Some climbers have been known to rip off all their clothes in the delusion that they are burning up when they are actually freezing to death.

Mariano noticed me take my gloves off and immediately walked over to me, knowing what was happening. At this point, I was actually in serious danger of getting frostbite, as I could no longer feel any sensation in my fingers. "I have to go back down! Right away!" I told him. "I'm an engineer. I can't lose my fingers, or I'm out of business."

Mariano started arguing with me, absolutely insistent that I could indeed continue if I could get my shit together. "Hey, aren't you the one who said you are climbing for the Nepali girls? Come on! You have to get up there! This is not about you! Aren't you doing this for those girls?" All the while, he was talking to me in a soft, calm, reassuring voice and rubbing my hands between his own, trying to get some sensation back into them. He put my gloves back on and then added a pair of over-mittens to further preserve some warmth. The dude saved my hands! I was so grateful to him, and I was excited that he would be our guide during a planned climb of Mount Kilimanjaro. Unfortunately, just a month before our scheduled departure for Africa, Mariano died in an avalanche with his climbing partner while attempting the ascent one of the most technically difficult Himalayan peaks in Pakistan. He was only thirty-seven years old.

The First Persian

We continued up, up, up, up. Every so often, I could hear the lead guide call out, "One hour to the top," trying to encourage us. Then "Thirty minutes to the summit." Then "Twenty minutes." We were getting closer and closer with every step, and this time I just knew I was going to make it to the top. And then—suddenly, it seemed—I was standing on top of the highest point in the Western and Southern Hemispheres. I could look around and see the whole world spread out before me. The whole Andes range was visible, running up the spine of the continent for hundreds of miles.

The view was majestic, gorgeous, and I was standing at 23,000 feet above sea level with roughly half the normal amount of oxygen in my gasping lungs. But most amazing of all to me was how good I was feeling. How was it possible that I had no headache or nausea? I was so proud of myself!

By contrast, the two guys from Dubai were suffering terribly, barely able to stand upright. They were sponsored by their government to climb the Seven Summits (the highest mountains on each of the continents), so they unfurled the UAE flag for the obligatory photograph. As I carefully unpacked the Empower Nepali Girls banner for posterity, I realized how jealous I was of their goal, which was so much more ambitious than my own. I wondered, for the first time, if maybe I could become the first Persian to accomplish such a thing, now that I'd knocked South America off the list. That would mean after Everest, I'd also have to hit Elbrus (Europe), Carstenz Pyramids (Oceania), Vinson (Antarctica), Kilimanjaro (Africa), and Denali (North America). The last one intimidated me even more than Everest because I'd be required to pull a sled that weighed as much as my own body for a month. Anyway, nice to have ambitious dreams.

Nobody was more surprised than I was that I had made it to the top. Given my past failures, I had just assumed I didn't have the stamina or the kind of body that could tolerate high altitudes. Given that I spent my whole life at sea level, that isn't a far stretch. But now that I had reached the summit, it felt like I had just fallen in love. I was incredibly happy. I started screaming into the wind, "I made it! I made it!"

I thought about the price I had paid for this joy. I was so exhausted and cold that I could barely remain erect. My face was swollen and sunburned. I'd lost all the weight that I had worked so hard to gain. After four months of diligent training, four months of abstaining from alcohol and other indulgences, all I could think about was getting back down the mountain and sampling some of the amazing Argentinian wines.

We all celebrated together once we arrived at the bottom. As exhausted as I felt, I was proud of what I'd accomplished: I was the first Persian woman to summit Aconcagua. To add to my excitement, our lead guide—who had kind of rolled his eyes when I had confided earlier that I intended to climb Everest—now he looked at me differently. "Have you ever heard of Aida?" he asked me.

"Aida?"

"*Si, ella es la primera mujer* ("Yes, she is the first woman") from Saudi Arabia to climb Everest."

I wondered why he was telling me this. I steeled myself, expecting another round of scolding, when he really surprised me. "But Sara, you are stronger than Aida. You actually did quite well on the mountain. Although you were tired, you had a lot of energy on the way down. And this whole time, you took care of your tentmate when she was having trouble, and you did so without complaint."

I was speechless and didn't quite know how to respond to that.

"Every time I looked back," he continued, "I saw you following me closely. You still have a lot of work left to do, but I think you will do it. *Tienes fuerte.* You are strong. You have, how you say, *buena tecnica*, good technique for someone so new to the sport. I think you are ready for what comes next, whatever that might be."

That was the very first time a professional climber encouraged me. That meant so much. Plus, now I was doing this for something so much bigger than myself.

Blowing in the Wind

After my experiences climbing in South America, I was feeling much more confident. I realized that if I could survive on Aconcagua for almost three weeks, I was getting stronger and more resilient. For the first time, I could actually imagine myself on Everest. I didn't know if I could make it to the top or not, but I was pretty sure I could give it a good try. *And maybe, just maybe,* the thought kept creeping into my mind, *I could even consider bagging a few of the other summits for charitable causes.*

I'd come a very long way during the past two years, remembering my initial naïve, feeble attempts on Whitney. Not only had my strength and conditioning improved significantly but I had also learned much about climbing, weather, the mountains, and even little tricks that experienced climbers take as second nature.

Following my return from Aconcagua, Jeffrey had just returned from Nepal on one of his visits with volunteers and team members. Jeffrey told me about his previous trip, during which a little girl who the foundation director, Pasang, had found abandoned in a Buddhist temple in Kathmandu. This five-year-old child, Nimsang, was lost and starving, so Pasang decided to bring her home and "adopt" her. Since then, Pasang and his wife had filled their home with other girls. The most recent one was an eight-year-old who had been sold to a family as a virtual slave. I eventually met this young girl, and I remember that while we were sitting at a table having a meal, she would surround her plate with her arms, as if she was afraid that someone would steal her food before she could put it in her mouth. I'm guessing that was how she was used to being treated.

When I heard about these children from Jeffrey, I felt helpless and heartbroken. It only renewed my commitment to do something really big in order to help them, even if it meant risking my own life. I felt more motivated than ever to complete this climb of Everest.

A Dream Come True

Sara
September 2014

It felt like everything I'd done so far in the mountains had been practice and rehearsal for the "real thing." Each of the climbs was targeted to test a particular skill set: acclimatization, conditioning, cold-weather adaptation, rappelling, avalanche safety, and a bunch of other things that I had learned, if not mastered. But now I was about to attempt a monster, the mystical mountain the Tibetans called "Turquoise Goddess," Cho Oyo. Even Edmund Hillary couldn't make it to the summit of the sixth-highest mountain in the world because of dangerous avalanches, not to mention Chinese army troops spotted in the region. It might not be K2 or Everest, but more than fifty climbers have died trying to get to the top.

Mind and Body

The closest mountain to my home, Mount Baldy, is "only" 10,000 feet, which sounds high until you consider it is only one-third the height of Everest. A few times each week, I would actually run up and down the peak, passing recreational hikers as if they were moving in slow motion. It was time to significantly increase my training regimen, so I signed up for a rigorous boot camp program with Bon, a personal trainer who was part drill sergeant and part motivational speaker. His job was to push me way beyond what I ever thought might be my limits.

I believed I was already in extraordinary shape, but Bon dispelled that notion during the first session. After fifteen minutes, I felt just as exhausted as after twenty days in the mountains. Every muscle ached after each intense session of weightlifting, rowing, indoor rock climbing, pulling a sled, then running or swimming, followed by yoga and stretching. Afterwards, I would just collapse.

"You think you're tired?" Bon would yell. "You have no idea what tired is until I'm done with you."

I could barely hear him: my heart was beating so hard my ears were vibrating.

"The way you work out here or what you do on the mountain is the way you live your life. If you give it all here, you give it all in the rest of your life."

I noticed a change in me once I began this training, one that seemed to affect many other things I was doing. I found myself committing myself more passionately to my teaching, fundraising, even my marriage which was starting to fall apart at the time because of the ways our interests were diverging. In just a few months, I gained an extra ten pounds of solid muscle, requiring me to buy new clothes. I couldn't wear any of my pants anymore.

My guides and trainers had convinced me that preparing my mind was just as important as preparing my body, so I also spent ten days at a silent meditation retreat center, where we were admonished to surrender all cravings and to accept that nothing is permanent. I wasn't quite ready to embrace all of that, but it was good practice to work on my mind. I never realized the self-discipline it would take to remain quiet for so long, focused only on meditation and reflection. This would prove extremely helpful during the challenges I would face that were more exercises of the mind than the body.

The part I was *most* excited about was that I'd be flying to Kathmandu first and would have a chance to finally meet the scholarship girls for the first time. Jeffrey had contacted the staff there to alert the children that I'd be arriving before we headed into China. He thought it would mean a lot to them to meet a woman who is a mountain climber. I asked Jeffrey what I should take with me for them, and he suggested just photos of my family and my life to show and inspire them. So I took my pictures of Iran, my apartment, my parents and siblings, my workouts in the gym, and the one of me holding the banner before the wind had blown it away.

I also felt a little more reassured because I'd "met" all of my teammates on social media. They seemed really friendly, spirited, and funny. I also learned there would be another woman, Laura, going with us who would be my tentmate. She was a mother with six children, and her goal was to climb the Seven Summits (like I was secretly contemplating). Remarkably, she had already scaled them all except Everest, which she had attempted to summit twice before but had had to turn back each time.

It turned out that Laura and I were on the same flight to Kathmandu, so I got a chance to connect with her at the gate at Los Angeles. I felt very reassured when I saw that she was as tiny as I am: we would be in this together.

So *This* is Nepal!

This was my first trip to Nepal, and I had no idea what I'd encounter except what Jeffrey had briefly told me about. Upon arrival, the airport looked like it was unfinished, just a single building and one runway. There were ancient Russian helicopters and military vehicles scattered around. I was also surprised to see a half dozen passenger jets parked near the solitary terminal, all of them from Middle Eastern countries. Since there were virtually no tourists or trekkers from Kuwait, the UAE, Saudi Arabia, Qatar, or Oman, I was quite perplexed until I learned that the planes were there solely to transport half a million Nepali workers to do the slave labor that residents refused to do. Thousands of them died each year because of poor health and safety conditions.

My first impression of the country was that everything seemed dusty and foggy. There were people everywhere, crowded in the streets, alleys, and shops. Even though I've spent a lot of time in the Middle East, nothing quite prepared me for the version of the Third World that exists in Nepal. Nothing seems to work quite right, with the constant strikes, delays, crazy traffic, power outages, political instability, and corruption, yet everyone seemed incredibly patient with it all.

The Nepali people make a gesture where they kind of waggle their heads side to side. At first, I thought they were saying "No" to me when I asked a question, but then I thought it meant "Yes" or even "Possibly." Now I realize it can mean any of these, but mostly it just means "Sure, whatever you want." I found the Nepali people to be the most accommodating, easygoing folks you could ever meet; you are constantly greeted by everyone—older people, shopkeepers, waiters, children, even babies—with "Namaste," which, roughly translated, means "The spirit within me honors the spirit within you." It's accompanied by hands forming a triangle under the chin as a demonstration of respect.

The drive from the airport was like something out of a crazy movie. There were no discernable traffic lanes. I'd see a motorcycle zipping by with a father driving, the mother sitting behind him with one child on her lap, another barely holding on to the back, and an infant perched on the handlebars. Another motorcycle zipped along with a goat on the driver's lap and a cage of chickens attached to the back.

On the particular day of my arrival, the driver explained that things were a little more congested and crazy than usual because it was a festival day.

"A special holiday?" I asked him. Laura wasn't paying much attention because she'd been to Kathmandu before, but she was staring out the window at a cow standing in the middle of the road blocking traffic. I also noticed there were police or soldiers standing around everywhere with machine guns, which I hoped weren't loaded.

The driver shook his head side to side, which I assumed was agreement. "Yes, it is a special holiday of Teej in which women pray to Lord Shiva for their husbands to have long lives. The women who are not yet married pray to Shiva that they might find husbands—"

"Wait a minute," I interrupted. "Only women do this for the men?" I wondered if this was the equivalent of our Father's Day.

"Yes, only women do this," he explained. "They wear red *saris* with *potes*. These are like glass, how do you say, seeds—no, beads—that glitter. And they fast all day."

"Wait," I interrupted once again. "Are you saying that women starve themselves all day so their husbands will—"

He made that head shake again.

I paused for minute, taking all this in. "Well, what about a day for men to honor women, so that they may live a long life? When is *that* festival?"

The driver shrugged. "There is no such day."

Ah, just like back in Iran, where women are second-class citizens. I wondered what the local people would think about Laura and me, two women from America who were going to climb their biggest mountains. And I wondered what the scholarship girls would think of me, a woman who looks like them but is not at all interested in being subservient to men or devoting my life solely to my husband's long life.

The Maze

Laura and I arrived at the Yak and Yeti Hotel after spending twenty-four hours crammed into airplane seats. As soon as we entered the lobby, we were greeted by a small, skinny guy who introduced himself as Lakpa, one of our guides.

He was so soft-spoken and deferential that you'd never guess that he is one of the most accomplished climbers in the world, having summited Everest more than a dozen times. I immediately felt drawn to him, so reassuring yet humble. When he smiled, he reminded me of Buddha.

Standing next to Lakpa was Marvin, another of our guides, who reminded me of a typical American mountaineer type you might see in a movie. He was wearing a flannel shirt and jeans, and he appeared strikingly handsome. He had half of a torn book with its cover missing in his hands. When I asked him about that, he laughed. "Hey," he explained, "no sense carrying any extra weight, right? Let me introduce you to the rest of the team, and then we need to do a gear check." Marvin was all business, quite a contrast to Lakpa's casual friendliness.

Laura and I were both exhausted and jetlagged, but Marvin insisted on going through our equipment before we could even get settled. He apologized for the abruptness but explained he didn't want to wait until we were in the "death zone" above 25,000 feet to discover that we were missing some item that could potentially save our lives.

"These are your climbing pants?" Marvin asked, pulling them out of my duffel with a look of distaste.

I nodded. What else could they be?

"These won't do at all."

"Excuse me?"

"They're not warm enough. We are going to be dealing with below-zero temperatures. So you're going to have to—"

"That's okay," Lakpa interrupted. "She's my size. She can borrow a pair of mine." Then he gave me one of his signature glorious grins. Marvin just shrugged, as if he was annoyed.

After unpacking and showering, Laura and I decided to go off exploring in the nearby tourist area called Thamel. This is where a lot of backpackers, ex-hippies, and trekkers on a budget hang out for cheap food, shopping, and seedy drug deals. Once we strolled over there, it really did remind me of what I imagined things must have been like during the '60s. There were lots of young people wandering around—mostly Germans, Scandinavians, and a few Australians. Every few steps, some shady characters approached us to sell their wares, ranging from cheap musical instruments and incense to hashish. I was greatly amused, but I could tell Laura was just annoyed by all the people continuously pestering us. Jeffrey told me that one time he was walking through here with a friend when a woman approached them with an infant. She thrust the baby in his friend's arms and started to back away. Jeffrey's friend had to run to follow the woman and give the baby back. Apparently, the mother was so desperate that she imagined her child would have a much better life with this foreigner. He also warned me about scams: a woman with a baby might approach us, ask us to buy some milk and food for them, and thank us gratefully, but then after we leave, return everything back to the store because the owner had actually hired them to reel in the tourists.

Thamel is my kind of place. It's crazy. It's crowded. Pedestrians, cars, scooters, bicycles, and rickshaws were everywhere on the narrow streets that were more like alleyways. Shops were crowded everywhere, with the owners calling out. There was the wafting smell of incense and weed, the sounds of Tibetan and Hindu music chants blaring from speakers. You could purchase *anything* here, and I loved bargaining with the people. Laura didn't much like it, so she asked me to do our negotiating. I'd had plenty of practice in Tehran, so I demonstrated my favored technique. The guy tells you his price, and you offer half of that. Then when he cuts it only 10 or 20 percent, you act disgusted and start to walk out of the store—very slowly. When he calls out to you to come back, you ignore him and continue on, but slowly so he can catch you. Then you tentatively agree to come back inside, perhaps have a cup of tea. And so it goes. It's all about the process, not just the price. This is a sacred tradition, one that I am both comfortable with and find endlessly amusing.

I'd been in Nepal only a few hours, and it felt like home to me. I loved the people. I loved all the activity and chaos. As we walked along the narrow alleys taking in all the sights and sounds, Laura and I started comparing notes on our prior climbs. Although she had much more experience, I realized that my own upbringing and culture allowed me to be her teacher as well while we navigated through this maze.

Holding Back Tears

Jeffrey had made arrangements for Pasang Sherpa, the director of the organization in Nepal, to pick me up and show me around the next morning. Pasang had been one of Jeffrey's first trekking guides, and he had always shown an interest in the work they had been doing with the children. Jeffrey confided to me that prior to Pasang taking over, his previous partner had neglected to pay debts that were due, neglected many of the children outside of his own ethnic group, and "redistributed" money to projects that bolstered his own standing in the community. In addition, he sexually harassed a few of the female staff, leading them to feel unsafe. As appalled as I was about this man's behavior, it was all familiar to me as the normal state of affairs in this part of the world. I was grateful that this guy had been replaced by someone who was honest and reliable.

The first thing that struck me about Pasang was his distinctive laugh. The thing that strikes *everyone* about Pasang is his laugh—frequent explosions of delight at almost everything, all the time, even at the most inopportune moments. There was a whole language to be translated from his laughing, which I soon learned to decode. Sometimes it meant something was truly amusing, but other times it could mean so many other things. Almost everything he said was punctuated with a laugh. This was just about the friendliest guy I'd ever met but also the most knowledgeable about his country. Jeffrey had told me much about him, as Pasang had been working with him for over a decade.

Although Pasang supports his family as a trekking guide, he also devotes a considerable part of his life to helping the girls. Babita, a social work student who was herself a scholarship girl, is a staff person for the organization and pretty much runs things along with Pasang, his family members, and friends. Babita has a room in Pasang's home along with other volunteers and even several scholarship girls who have nowhere else to live. Over time, "Babi" would take on more and more responsibility for the daily work, since it was important that women have a more visible role in an organization that seeks to empower girls.

Pasang was accompanied by several children, including his daughter Chhusang, age sixteen, and Nimsang, the little girl I mentioned earlier who he had found abandoned on the street. While we were driving back to his home, the girls asked me if I was familiar with any famous Nepali or Indian actresses. There was an instant bond between us because growing up in Iran, I was indeed quite knowledgeable about Bollywood songs and films, so we started singing together the whole way. Pasang just kept laughing while he pointed out sights along the way.

Finally, we arrived wherever we were going. I saw these two big blue doors that started to open as we got out of the car. We had been driving on this bumpy, rocky road, squeezed between walls that were so narrow that only one vehicle could slip by at a time. I looked through the doors of what I figured must be the entrance to a school and saw two long lines of children that had formed. They were organized by age and size, with little ones—perhaps only three or four years old—standing first. I could see they were all holding out their hands with flowers in them, and as I walked through this gauntlet, each child placed flowers in my hands or a *khata*, a sacred scarf blessed by the Dalai Lama, around my neck. Each child greeted me with *"Namaste"* or "Welcome, ma'am." I couldn't help but break out in tears of joy. You just can't imagine what it feels like to be so honored by children you have just met.

Apparently, the children had been told who I was and why I was there. They knew I was an engineer and a mountaineer who was going to climb Everest, but they'd also been told I was a volunteer and fundraiser for the organization that raises money to support the poorest girls in their school. I was trying to smile and show my gratitude to the children, but all I could think to do was to keep telling myself, "Don't cry. Keep it together." I just wanted to stop and hold all the children. I wanted to tell them that I would do my very best to help them. It felt like my whole life was changing in that moment, that I would never be the same. So far, everything I knew about these girls and what the foundation was doing was from second-hand stories told to me by Jeffrey and others. But now this was real. I looked at these girls' gorgeous, smiling faces and realized that their actual lives depended on me. It was impossible to hold back the tears.

Sharing My Story

I sat in a circle with dozens of the scholarship girls, the oldest (who was perhaps twelve or thirteen) as well as younger ones who couldn't have been more than four or five. Babita introduced herself to me, and I was surprised how poised and in charge she was. Pasang had gone off to huddle with the school principal and teachers, leaving us alone. It was Babita who organized everything, and I could see the girls adored her. She was the model of everything they wanted to be some day. In some ways, she was an example of who I hoped to be someday as well—devoted to serving others.

I was asked to tell the girls about myself, so I explained where I came from and what my job is in America—that I'm an electrical engineer and computer scientist and I teach at a university. I could see that some of the girls weren't exactly sure what to make of that, how a woman who looked like them could have a man's job. Then I told them about my plan to bring greater attention to their needs by first climbing Cho Oyo, followed by Everest, and perhaps others after that. Some of the girls' mouths dropped open, immediately covered by their hands; others just giggled, as if this was some kind of fantasy story.

Babita asked the girls to introduce themselves to me, and it wasn't at all what I expected. They had memorized a simple introduction in English. "My name is Amita. I am in Class Three," one girl would say. "My parents' names are Amaya and Sunita. I have two brothers. Their names are Sandesh and Sajit." As they would recite this carefully rehearsed speech, they would look down at their feet because they were so shy.

I squatted down by each one of them and said, "Please look at me. Don't look down. Be proud of who you are. You are smart. You will do great things. I will help you." As I was saying these words, I felt so shy myself. I felt so overwhelmed and out of my element. I didn't know what I was supposed to do or say. Jeffrey hadn't prepared me for this part.

After we went through this awkward series of introductions, I started showing the girls some photos that I'd brought along. When I pointed out my husband, Matt, they all started giggling. But by that time, the ice seemed to have been broken, and they started asking me questions about how I had become an engineer, whether girls can do that in America, and why I wanted to climb mountains. Jeffrey had already told me that except for Sherpas who are specifically paid as guides, most Nepali people don't really understand why tourists and trekkers come so far just to walk in the mountains. For them, the trails are the only highways to get from one place to another, and they are grueling, steep, and difficult to navigate while carrying heavy loads. It doesn't strike them as much fun.

I thought for a long minute before answering. "Well," I said after the long pause, "unless we push ourselves to do things that are really hard and face challenges that frighten us, we can never really know what we are capable of doing. Do you know what I mean?"

I saw their heads nod. I wasn't sure, at first, how much English they actually understood, but I could see absolute clarity in the faces of the older girls. "Climbing mountains," I continued, "is about facing hardships for me. It's a way for me test myself."

Again, they nodded, or rather waggled, their heads. This time I could tell they agreed.

"Many people have told me that what I do is not the sort of thing for a girl to attempt. They say it's too hard and that I should stay home and have babies."

The girls covered their mouths and giggled, but I could tell immediately that they got it, the message I was telling them. They gathered around me even closer, a few of the little ones competing to sit on my lap, some others leaning over my shoulders. I so badly wanted them to know that they could do this too. They could follow in my footsteps and pursue their own dreams.

They asked so many wonderful questions. How did I come to the United States? What was it like living in Iran when I was a child? How did I go to university, and why did I decide to study engineering? What did I think of their country so far? I laughed at the last question because I'd been in Nepal for less than twenty-four hours, but I patiently answered anything they wanted to know about me. They were especially surprised that I didn't get married until I was in my late twenties and still didn't have any children yet. I explained that first there were things I wanted to do in my life, that I hadn't gotten married until I finished my education and had a good career and that I didn't want to have children until I first finished other things in my life that were important to me. I could tell that this interested them but sure didn't fit with their own cultural values: girls as young as fifteen years old might be expected to marry, and hitting eighteen without a husband must have seemed strange to them.

"There's no hurry," I told them. "It's better to finish your education so you can take care of yourself and your family *before* you get married. That way, you will never be dependent on a man."

"Like Jeffrey Sir's students?" one of the girls blurted out, then seemed embarrassed for interrupting me.

"What do you mean?" I asked, puzzled by the question.

"The students that he brings here," another girl explained. "They are already old, even though they are students. Some are even twenty-five already and they don't have husbands."

I smiled at how strange that seemed to them but just encouraged the girl to continue. "Yes?" I prompted.

"Well, they tell us something like what you said. That in their country girls don't get married until they are done with school. Sometimes they even wait until they have jobs." All the girls were nodding in astonishment at the very idea of that.

"And one girl, she told us that she might *never* get married. She said she didn't need a man to make her happy."

I explained to the girls that, yes, this was normal where I was from, that many women see themselves as equal to men in every way. Then I told them that I was a better engineer, professor, and mountain climber than most of the men I'd ever known. They all laughed at that.

One girl who looked about fourteen piped up after that. "Excuse me, ma'am, but I have friends and know other girls who have boyfriends, and they want to get married. My father, he tells me that I should get married too. He says that girls don't belong in school anyway. What should I do?"

I had no idea what to say to her. I knew Jeffrey fielded these kinds of questions all the time and had been doing this for years. He's a psychologist and all, but I'd only been here a day, and I was used to solving problems as an engineer. I had no solution to this problem. All I could think to do was waggle my head the way that they do and say, "Yes," "No," and "Maybe." I needed time to figure that one out.

They were all staring at me, waiting for some other gems of wisdom, so I told them more about my life when I was younger. "Although I'm now thirty-three years old, when I was younger, I fell in love with a boy."

Again, they tried to stifle their giggles as they looked at one another.

"There is much pressure in my culture too for girls to marry when we are young. But there are many things I wanted to see and know, and I knew those experiences would end once I was married."

One of the older girls suddenly stood up, as if she was about to leave. "Well, my parents want me to marry my cousin. They are forcing me, and there's nothing I can do about that." Then she turned and walked away. It just broke my heart, but I tried to keep my attention on the girls still around me.

It seemed to be intermission when one of the teachers in the school came by with a tray of cookies and a thermos of milk tea, their national drink. Everywhere I would visit in Nepal, we would be offered variations of this tradition, whether it was tea with milk, *chai* tea with various spices like cardamom, cinnamon, and ginger, or Sherpa tea with the even more unusual ingredients of yak butter and salt.

I was starving because it was lunchtime and I hadn't yet eaten anything because of the time difference from back home. The children politely refused the refreshments for reasons unclear to me other than I was their guest, so I shoveled down a few cookies, drained the mug of tea, and then turned back to them.

"How about let's play a game? I've noticed that when you introduced yourself to me, you were very shy. Your voices were so soft I could barely hear you. And you memorized something to say to me, but it probably wasn't what you really wanted me to know about you. So, how about this: Everyone stand up and form a circle. When I point to you, I want you to look me straight in the eyes and speak up. I want you to use a loud, confident voice and tell me something about yourself that is important. I don't care what it is, anything you want. And you can tell me in English or Nepali, it doesn't matter. I don't care what you say, but I want you to say it loudly, confidently, looking at me the whole time."

Hey, I was just winging it. I was used to teaching college students—mostly all men who were studying to be engineers—so this was *way* out of my own comfort zone. To my surprise, they *loved* this game. Every time I pointed to one of them, they would talk to me in a strong voice. Most of the time I had no idea what exactly they were saying to me, but they had fun doing it. I realized that although I had come to Nepal to climb Cho Oyo, after just one day, it felt like I'd already accomplished enough that I could have gone home a happy woman.

We took "selfies" of one another and then a group photo before I had to say goodbye. I promised I would return to them in six weeks after I climbed the mountain.

Home Visits

Before I returned to the other world of climbers waiting for me at the hotel, Pasang and his family took me out for a meal to try *dal bhat* for the first time. This is the national dish—rice and lentils, usually accompanied with curried vegetables—that Nepalis eat twice each day. It's often the *only* thing they eat because it is considered so nutritious and inexpensive. Let's just say it is an acquired taste.

Pasang and Babita had arranged for me to visit a few more of the scholarship girls in their homes. They thought I might like to meet some of the families and to see how the girls live. The first place we stopped was a small hut, maybe the size of a small hotel room. There was a young mother there, maybe in her late teens, and she had two little girls; one was three years old, and the older girl was five. When I asked where the father was, the mother just shrugged. Apparently, he had gone to an Arabic country to find work and was never heard from again. They didn't know if he had died or had simply abandoned their family. This was a very common scenario in which laborers are exported to do manual labor that the local citizens of Middle Eastern countries consider beneath them. The workers are restricted to camps and risk their lives in construction or maintenance jobs in 120-degree temperatures every day in order to send money home.

We walked to another house where there was an eight-year-old scholarship girl. As we sat and talked, she told me she enjoyed math as her favorite class. I asked if I could see her schoolwork. This girl was incredibly smart, like a little jewel hidden away in this desolate little place with no resources. The scholarship girls are children who consider the opportunity to attend school and study as a privilege. In Nepal, unlike in the United States and other countries, students must have a uniform and school supplies, plus they have to pay tuition to attend even public school.

While I was sitting with the family, I had this vivid flashback of being back in Iran. I remembered I was about ten years old, and it was the Persian New Year. There was a knock on the door of our home, and we were sitting around because there was no school that day. I opened the door, and standing there were some of my teachers. I was so surprised I just stood there with my mouth open, thinking I was in some kind of trouble.

"May we come in?" one of the teachers asked, seeing my look of surprise and confusion. I just nodded my head and shyly backed away. Thoughts were racing through my head of all the things I might have done wrong. I just knew that I must have done something really bad for all of them to come to my house like this, especially on a holiday.

I couldn't have been more wrong. The teachers just wanted my parents to know how smart I was and what a capable student I had become. As we sat and had tea together, just like I was doing with this girl in Nepal, they asked me all sorts of questions about my life, what subjects I liked best, and every little detail about our house. I remembered that so vividly as I was sitting in this hut, and I recalled what a huge impression that had on me for the rest of my life. That was one of the first times—maybe *the* first time— that I realized I had a special gift, one that my teachers wished to support and nourish. It meant so, so much to me, and it made me want to work even harder.

Now I was the one who was trying to inspire and support this girl who was so incredibly gifted as well and didn't quite realize it. I could feel myself starting to lose control, so I abruptly excused myself and ran outside sobbing. It was as if this little girl was me—and I was her. I realized in that moment that I might have the same impact on these children as my teachers once had on me by showing how much they cared and supported me.

When I came back inside, pretending I had had to use the toilet, I was composed once again. I turned to the mother and thanked her for being so strong and for supporting her daughter's education. "You must be so proud that she is so smart. She is going to do important things in her life with your help, with *all* of our help." I explained to her that we were going to support her daughter in school as far as she could go. We would provide a scholarship and enough financial support for her to continue her education to study engineering, like me, or perhaps medicine.

The mother held up her hands to her chin in the familiar sign of respect, and she broke out in the most glorious smile. "*Dheri dhanyabahd*, thank you so much for giving my daughter something that was never given to me." Then she reached out to hold my hands.

This conversation and experience were repeated a half dozen times that afternoon. In each case, the family welcomed me with tea and biscuits. I visited homes where five people lived in the space the size of a large closet, sometimes the parents and one child sleeping together on a pallet on the floor. The kitchen was just a little portable stove on the ground. I reminded myself that I would never have the right to complain about anything in my life ever again.

By the time we returned to the hotel, I was an emotional wreck, not to mention exhausted from the time change and the overwhelming day. While my teammates had been enjoying a day's rest—shopping, touring the city, loading up on pizza and beer—I had been immersed in this invisible world that climbers and trekkers never see, never know exists. But there was no better "training" I could ever have done to prepare for the next six weeks in the Himalayas. Now I *knew* why I was doing this. I had a reason that dwarfed anything else I could ever have imagined. When things got tough, when I wanted to give up, I would just remember these girls and how much they were depending on me to bring attention to their plight. It was now my life's mission to be their role model, to show them what a woman can do.

Preparations and Training

Sara
October 2014

My heart was pounding so hard I could feel vibrations throughout my body. I tried to take deep breaths, but I was still gasping for air, trying to suck as much oxygen as I could into my lungs. Just when I thought I'd calmed down, I'd take another few steps and end up gasping once again. It felt like I was slowly suffocating, which I suppose was exactly the case.

Each day we were scheduled to do acclimatization hikes at progressively higher altitudes. The best strategy for adapting to life so far above sea level is to make sure you don't climb too far too fast so as to allow the body to adjust to significantly decreased oxygen levels. The depth of respiration decreases, requiring the production of more red blood cells and increased pressure in the pulmonary arteries, which circulate hemoglobin. This is designed to counteract the deficit in the oxygen that is needed to power muscles. Given that climbers are usually working at maximum capacity much of the time, there is also greater risk that terrible things—like pulmonary or cerebral edema—can happen and can easily become fatal.

During these training climbs, I got to know my group members a bit better. I had been a little worried because a few of the men were so much taller and bigger than I was, requiring me to match their longer strides during climbs. But before long, I was reassured that we would all take care of one another. That's one of the remarkable outcomes of expeditions like this. Boundaries collapse. Masks come down. With our very lives at stake the relationships among team members become more authentic and honest in ways that rarely happen back home. In one sense, that's just as important to me as the climbing itself.

It's the stories you hear while on a climbing expedition that partially make the suffering so endurable. Several of our guides had scaled many 8,000-meter peaks all over the world, escorting fabulously wealthy clients and eccentric adventurers. They regaled us with tales about one older guy in his sixties who fell in love with a twenty-year-old and decided to divorce his wife while on the trip. Another rich guy decided he was worried about how his heart would hold up, so while on an Everest expedition, he decided he needed to see his cardiologist back home in Los Angeles. Once he was examined and told his heart was just fine, he hopped back on a plane, flew back to Kathmandu, and hired a helicopter back to Everest Base Camp. Now *that's* some acclimatization trip, going from sea level to 18,000 feet in just a few days.

As we ascended higher and higher toward Base Camp, the routines for each day were much the same: long hikes during the day, then descend back down and sit by the stove to dry our socks. There was plenty of time to think about things—about life, about priorities, about loved ones—sometimes *way* too much time. And yet there is something altogether different when on a climb like this. Back home, at least in Southern California, everyone is busy all the time with their work and responsibilities. People live so far from one another that it is somewhat rare that friends and family get together and just hang out, without the distractions of a television or mobile device. During these conversations, I revealed to others why I was actually doing this climb: not just to prepare for Everest but to show all the girls what is possible if you are willing to work hard enough.

I could tell the other team members were intrigued by my mission to join them. This wasn't just an individual triumph for me but rather I represented a whole community of others I was supporting. They asked so many questions about what we were doing in Nepal, just across the border. They had seen for themselves the poverty and deprivation that were so pervasive. They had noticed all the children standing along the side of the trail, watching them as they marched by on their way to the next destination. I could tell that I was making them feel a little uncomfortable, if not guilty, because their own motives were so personal, if not self-centered. And yet they were intensely interested in what I was doing and wondered how they could help.

First View

I woke up really early one morning, way before sunrise, because we'd been told that if it was clear, we would be able to see the north side of Everest. Of course I'd already studied every contour of the mountain on maps, Google

Earth, and photographs, but for the first time, I could actually see the fabled peak that was calling to me poking out of the clouds below.

I was in awe. It looked so unreachable. The south side was completely white with snow, but I could see the north side was jagged, rocky, ominous. I tried to imagine myself standing on top of the tallest peak in the world, but it seemed beyond me. I shook my head and turned around to face the mountain in front of me. *Enough for today. We'll see what tomorrow brings.*

We left that day for Base Camp, which I expected would look like a village of mountain climbers but instead resembled an army camp, with Chinese soldiers standing around with their guns and giving orders not to take photos. We pretty much ignored them: What were they going to do, shoot us?

As we toured the camp, I could see the summit of Cho Oyu, with its distinctive flat top looming high above us. We made the rounds visiting the tents of the other climbing teams from around the world, and I was surprised to meet another Iranian, a doctor from San Francisco, who was just as shocked to see me.

"What are *you* doing here?" he blurted out. "Shouldn't you be at a shopping mall looking for boots and a leather jacket?"

I supposed he didn't mean to be so rude, but he was talking about the stereotype of Persian girls from wealthy families in Southern California. He also displayed the typical attitude of men from my country that I had grown accustomed to, although he seemed to thaw a bit when I explained to him why I was really there: not for myself, but to help others.

There was even more free time at Base Camp than in the teahouses because we needed recovery days after climbing high to further acclimatize. And when you are living in a tent city, there isn't much privacy, since you are all living virtually on top of one another.

That evening, there was a full moon on a perfectly clear, cold night. As I was lying in my tent, I could see the shadow of a yak so close that it looked like he was standing right outside. I thought about opening the flap to look outside and see if I needed to take defensive measures, but I was too scared to move. So I just stayed up all night, gripping my ice axe in case I needed to protect myself.

Up and down. Up and down. That was my life. We'd climb higher and higher, conditioning our bodies to the thin air and steep climbs, and then we'd descend back down to rest and recover. During one of our frequent social gatherings, a few people at the table asked me what I was going to do next. That always seems to be a frequent topic of conversation among climbers, no matter what mountain you are on: What are you going to do after this one?

At first, I was reluctant to admit my plans to others outside my intimate group because I didn't want to hear any more doubts and criticism from people. But I'd come to like and trust those around me; they were accepting and understanding toward *anything* that anyone chose to reveal about themselves. So I confided to them that I was on Cho Oyu to prepare for Everest. Laura was already aware of my detailed plans because we'd stayed up late at night talking in our tent about all kinds of things, and I already knew that she was thinking about Everest next year as well. We'd even talked about possibly doing it together if our schedules worked out.

After my disclosure, almost everyone else said that Everest was a dream of theirs as well but one they admitted was likely unrealistic, given the exorbitant cost and the amount of time they'd have to take off from their jobs. Lakpa and Marvin then started telling many stories about their Everest climbs: how different it is from what we were doing because of the special equipment and gear that was needed and how much more difficult it would be because of the icefall, the ladders, and the sheer numbers of other climbing teams that were all competing for priority on the ropes. I remained mostly quiet during the discussion, listening as carefully as I could, but I could tell that some of the others looked at me differently after that—they could tell this wasn't just a casual lark for me but a mission I was taking very seriously.

Laura and I were becoming attached to one another, quite literally. Sleep at high altitude is intermittent and sketchy at best, and I constantly woke up several times in the middle of the night—that is, when I could sleep at all. Sometimes I found that during the night I had rolled over and was practically sleeping on top of Laura or had somehow ended up on her side of the tent. More often, she was so sweet and kind that I didn't have the heart to tell her that we were all tangled up, so I reassured her that she was the best tentmate ever. You just can't imagine the things you have to put up with, being crowded into such close quarters. Depending on what one has for dinner, passing gas can be so out of control you can barely gasp for air in the already limited oxygen available. Sometimes we had to leave the tent flap open to get some air circulation going, but then because it was so cold outside, we would be freezing all night.

Advanced Base Camp

My climbing style is, to be perfectly honest, a little unusual. I like to listen to music while on the mountain, especially favorite Persian songs that are so irresistible that I can't help but dance in the middle of my steps. I move my arms in that hypnotic rhythm and stutter step my feet in a very rough approximation of moves I can make easily without heavy boots and crampons. I don't ever realize I'm doing this, but the others on my team are usually quite amused by it. Sometimes, when I'm alone—or *think* I'm alone—on top of a ridge, I'll turn up the volume and really start moving and swaying to the music. I feel self-conscious about this, worried that my guides will scold me for wasting energy but I find the dancing relaxes and soothes me.

As we headed to higher elevations, I could definitely feel myself becoming stronger. So far, so good. The next day, as we hiked up to ABC (Advanced Base Camp), Marvin carefully checked each of us out, asking how we were doing, assessing our fitness and readiness to go so much higher. Most of us already had headaches and insomnia. Laura, in particular, hadn't been sleeping at all which isn't that unusual.

Finally, the guides told us we had arrived at the destination, but I had to take their word for it because I could barely see past my own goggles. One minute it was still and quiet; the next brought a blizzard. The wind suddenly picked up at ferocious velocity, followed by a blinding snowstorm that was coming at us more horizontally than vertically. It is terrifying to be standing in a complete whiteout, unable to even determine up from down.

As soon as we stopped, I unpacked every item of clothing that I carried with me, layering all my fleece and my puffy jacket and pants. Even outfitted like a big balloon, I was still wet and freezing. I walked around in the increasingly deep snow, as much to stay warm as to tour our new home. I could see that the porters from another team had set up tents already; all of our equipment and supplies were arriving by yaks a few hours later.

We were graciously invited by members of the other team to warm ourselves in one of their tents, and they offered us hot drinks. As usually happens in such situations, we traded stories with one another about where we'd been and where we were going next. There was one woman climber with the other team, Christina, who seemed especially interested to know who I was and what I was doing. When I told her about our work supporting the girls and that I was climbing to raise money for them, she wanted to know everything about our program. I noticed, at this point, that everyone else had stopped talking to listen to what I was saying.

I looked around the tent at the thirty other climbers who were all watching me with interest when I described what I'd been doing ten days before, visiting the children in their homes. I would later learn that literally thousands of climbers pass right by some of our scholarship girls standing along the Everest trail (easily recognizable by their bright puffy jackets that we provide for them), and hardly anyone ever stops to talk to them.

The group seemed so interested in what I was doing, or perhaps they were just happy to be talking about anything other than the weather, the routes, and complaints about the food, cold, and inevitable delays. During one of the pauses, I heard one voice ask me, fairly aggressively, "Aren't your parents worried about you?"

Of course, it was the Persian doctor from San Francisco who I'd met earlier and had been giving me a hard time.

"Excuse me?" I said, dumbfounded about where *that* came from.

"Your parents. And your husband. Do they let you climb mountains like this?"

"*Let* me?" This guy was really getting under my skin. Or maybe I was just annoyed because he reminded me of so many other men from back home.

"Yes. I know Persian parents. And I don't think many of them would be happy about you doing this, being here."

I so badly wanted to ask him if his parents or his wife let him climb mountains, but instead I just smiled sweetly and ignored him. The timing was perfect when one of our guides stuck his head inside the door to tell us that our equipment had finally arrived.

A Prayer to the Gods

Sara
September–October 2014

I felt a little better the next morning, although I had still barely slept more than an hour or two. As I've said, this is normal at high altitude, but it doesn't make things easier to endure, wrestling around all night in tight quarters. During the few times I actually fell asleep, I awakened gasping for air and completely disoriented.

Since we were soon to begin the serious climbing, we had a Puja ceremony scheduled, during which we were instructed to beseech the gods for safe passage. This is a Sherpa tradition, especially among those of them who are monks. Sometimes an eldest son might be sent to a monastery as a child for religious instruction and to serve the lama, the spiritual leader. If economic hardship within the family becomes untenable, the monk may then be granted permission to earn money as a guide to help support his family. There were several such Sherpas in our group who would lead the ceremony.

A small altar wrapped in colorful prayer flags had been created. As the monks chanted their prayers, we were each asked to reverently place our crampons and ice axe on top of the rocks in order to bless them for the climb. I also placed the Empower Nepali Girls flag on top and made sure it was clearly visible. Then we presented symbolic gifts to all the gods respected by those present: Hindu, Buddhist, Christian, and Muslim among them. Incense was burned, and then we each threw a handful of rice as an offering. As a last part of the ceremony, we each rubbed flour on one another's faces as a personal blessing.

I realized as I was watching the proceedings that this wasn't really about climbing at all or even some superstitious belief that this would somehow protect us from harm. This was a ritual about respect for the mountain, about the uncertainties of life, and about reflective meditation regarding the meaning of our actions.

Walking Zombie

Today we were carrying some of our equipment up to Camp One—21,000 feet. I decided to leave as much as possible behind in my tent to lighten my pack, heavier than I could comfortably manage. It took us ten hours to get there and back, and the whole time it was snowing. The last hour before we arrived at Camp One, I was seriously regretting my decision to lighten my pack because I was freezing with limited clothes. I decided to forget about the summit; I just wanted to go back down where it was warm and headache free. Every second, I was asking myself why the hell I was doing this. Every single step, I was trying to convince myself to take just one more before I turned around.

I was so tired that at one point, I felt an abrupt jolt and realized that I had actually fallen asleep as I was walking! I realized how dangerous this was because there were so many deep crevasses crisscrossing our route, and one small mistake would send me careening down into nothingness. By then I was seriously concerned because I wondered how I would recover from such a lapse of attention as we got higher, the slopes got steeper, and the dangers became so much more unforgiving.

In and out of my reverie, which at times felt like hallucinations, I started thinking about an older woman I'd read about who, at sixty-four years of age, managed to swim from Cuba to Florida. She had to deal with so many horrible things during the 110-mile marathon, which took something like fifty straight hours in the water. There were huge waves she had to swim through, blowing winds, stings from numerous jellyfish, and the threat of sharks, not to mention having to exert herself like that for two straight days. It seemed insane, especially considering how old she was. But she was my inspiration, and I imagined her watching me. I could also almost hear her talking to me, encouraging me to keep going. "Remember," I could hear her saying inside my head, "you picked this goal. Nobody made you do this. It's bigger than you. This isn't about you anyway. It's for the girls. Remember why you are doing this. Remember the people counting on you."

I'd like to say that this counsel made all the difference, but whatever inspiration and encouragement I felt from the ghost of this woman living inside my head lasted only a few steps longer before I thought about giving up once again. Then I remembered what it was like on Aconcagua and how finally reaching the summit was one of the best days of my life. Sure, it wasn't nearly as hard as this monster, but that experience reminded me once again why the goal was so worth the effort. For some reason, I was able to hold on to that feeling until we finally reached the high camp.

A More Positive Attitude

After descending back down from that first climb up to Camp One, we were given a rest day to recover, and wow, did we need it. Almost everyone had headaches, sore throats, and flu-like symptoms. I had totally lost it trying to get up to 21,000 feet, so I wondered how I could possibly handle another 6,000 feet to get to the top of Cho Oyu, much less the 8,000 additional feet to summit Everest. I think at that moment, if I'd had the strength to get out of my tent, I would have tracked down Marvin or Lakpa and insisted that someone escort me back down. But that would have required more energy than I could muster, so I just wallowed in my misery and hoped I could finally fall asleep.

During the night, I dragged myself out of my sleeping bag, completely forgetting that I had decided to quit the day before. Although I hadn't gotten much sleep, this time it wasn't because of fatigue, aches and pains, or the altitude. I had left some of my gear at Camp One, including my pee bottle, the one I use during the night with a funnel so I don't have to leave the tent and brave the frigid cold. I remembered Laura saying that holding your pee brings down your body temperature. Because I was under strict orders to keep drinking water, there was no way I'd be able to hold it in during the night, which required me having to go outside at about 2:00 a.m. I opened the tent flap, crawled outside, and looked up at the most spectacular view I'd ever seen: stars so bright and numerous that they blanketed the sky. I was so taken with the experience that I started to return to my tent until I realized I had forgotten why I was out there in the first place.

Once settled back inside, waiting for sleep to hit me, I started reviewing all that I had learned about keeping a positive attitude, especially during adversity. Mountain climbing is as much a mental effort as a physical activity. It's about tolerating difficulties without feeling discouraged. It's about being disciplined and focused. But mostly, it is about staying upbeat, especially when things get really, really tough. I realized that if I could do this, if I could really drag myself up to the summit, anything else I did in life back home would seem easy by comparison.

The really strange thing was how mercurial and unpredictable my moods had become. One minute I was ready to surrender, and the next I was feeling fearless. I was in the throes of ecstasy, watching the spectacular stars at night, then a bit later I was crying myself to sleep because I was so miserable. I needed to somehow stay more grounded and to stop overreacting to every little obstacle along the way. I needed to keep more positive energy flowing, so I practiced my meditation as a way to relax and remain clear. The next thing I knew, it was morning, and I'd had the best sleep I could ever remember having in a long time. I felt renewed and bursting with energy. My cramps were gone. No more nausea or headache.

Notebooks from Beyond

I suppose there are a lot of possible explanations for my sudden change in attitude. Perhaps it was because my body had finally adapted to the altitude, or I'd finally gotten the rest I needed, or whatever malady infecting me had run its course, but I preferred another theory. I'm not a conventionally religious person. In some ways, I'm quite skeptical of orthodox traditions, which you could certainly appreciate, since I grew up with all the oppression by religious leaders in Iran. But I have always believed in some kind of divine or spiritual power that emanates from somewhere in the universe.

I don't mean to sound all New Age, but I remembered one incident that occurred when I was studying at UCLA. I had little money and very few resources in college, so I lived in one of the dumpiest apartments you can imagine. The building was such a wreck that the windows wouldn't open, and hardly anything worked properly. I didn't even have any furniture, and I could barely afford to eat anything other than noodles.

It was my first day of classes, and I hadn't yet figured out a way to buy any supplies for school, including notebooks to record lectures. I showed up at my first class and sat next to a girl who had a collection of a half dozen color-coded, seemingly customized notebooks in bright primary colors. When she saw me looking curiously at her stack of books, she just shrugged. "It's my dad," she said apologetically. "He bought them for me."

I turned away, wishing I had a father who would help me get settled in school. During the previous few days, I had seen so many parents helping their kids move into their apartments, taking them out for meals, and walking with them around town while they shopped for things. My family was back in Arizona and couldn't really help me with anything financially, so I was completely on my own. The girl noticed I had nothing on my desk, so she asked me if I wanted one of her notebooks. I just shook my head and tried not to cry. I felt such deep sadness and thought of my father, my real father, who died before I was born. I imagined that if he were there with me, he could take me out to buy notebooks and other things I needed. For now, I'd have to make do with the few sheets of paper I had borrowed from the girl next to me.

After class, I was walking back to my dismal apartment when I heard this noise that startled me. It was the "beep, beep" sound of a truck backing up, and I saw that it was pulling into an alley just in front of me, blocking my way. I had been so lost in my own thoughts, feeling sorry for myself, that I almost walked smack into it.

The driver got out of the truck, and for a minute, I thought he was going to yell at me for almost getting hit by his vehicle. But instead, he walked around to the back of the truck, opened the door, and started yelling in a loud voice, "Notebooks. Free notebooks. Who wants some notebooks?"

Are you kidding me? This was awesome! What I wanted most in the world at that moment were notebooks, and who pulls up but this guy offering to give them away for free—and for no reason that I could figure out, unless they were advertising something they wanted to distribute. But hey, beggars can hardly complain.

"Hey, I'll take one!" I yelled out to him. I was so excited I could hardly stand it. This was downright weird, and it was about to become much more so.

"Take as many as you want," he said with a smile and placed a pile of them in my arms, all different colors. But here was the *really* amazing part. I glanced at the cover of the notebooks and saw, emblazoned right on the front, the word "safari.com."

That's my name! Of all the coincidences imaginable, not only does this guy show up with a truck of notebooks just when I needed them, but it was as if they were specifically designed just for me! It was spooky. But it also renewed my faith that forces beyond what we can possibly understand appear during those times of our greatest need.

I know this sounds really strange, and I'm a little embarrassed to admit this, but I felt—no, I *knew*—that these notebooks were from my dad. I started sobbing as I walked home, and I said a prayer to my long-dead father, whom

I'd never actually met. "Thank you, Father, for taking care of me. Thank you for being there for me when I needed you the most."

So as I woke up from my first good night's sleep feeling completely refreshed, almost reborn, I just nodded to myself in acknowledgment. I found myself thinking about how those notebooks arrived when I most needed them and wondered if there was some divine intervention (or luck) once again to rescue me. I don't know if this time it was my father's energy, a guardian angel that had shown up again, those in my meditation group back home, or the spirit of the girls I was supporting, but *something* was very different, and even though I couldn't explain it, I was very grateful.

The Ice Cliff

It was like I was vibrating. And it was two o'clock in the morning. I'd eaten so many protein bars and B12 vitamins that I doubted I would ever sleep that night, with all the energy in my system. My knees were still pulsating from the caffeine I'd consumed, the lack of oxygen, the excitement, or something else. It was scaring me because my legs wouldn't stop wiggling, as if they had a life of their own and weren't even connected to me at all. I wondered if I should wake up a guide and tell him what was happening. Maybe it meant I was dying. I tried to listen to music to calm down, but the battery was dead because of the cold. I took the battery out and put it in my underwear to try to warm it up. After about a half hour, I tried again, and it lasted long enough to play one song. It was 4:00 a.m., but we still had hours to go.

The night seemed endless, but finally it started to get light, and I knew we had an important day ahead of us. For the first time, we would be tackling the most technical part of the climb, an ice wall that required us to use our crampons and ice axes. It was slow going for sure, especially because we needed time to get into a rhythm and work as a team. Much of the way, all I could think about was the chocolate bar I had been saving for when I needed it most: *this* was going to be that special occasion. I was actually hungry for the first time in a while. I had skipped dinner because they were serving MREs (meals ready-to-eat), which are what soldiers eat when they are on the battlefield. They were so disgusting that I had just settled for a handful of almonds, and I couldn't wait to get at the chocolate bar.

After several hours of climbing, we took a break to rest for a few minutes. I immediately took off my pack and started digging into my bag for the treat, setting things aside, balancing one of my two water bottles on the ledge while I searched further. Success! Just as I grabbed the chocolate bar at the bottom of a pocket, my pack touched the water bottle, and I watched with horror as it tipped over the edge and rolled down the glacier. Lakpa, always quick on his feet, started to run after it but then thought better of the idea when the bottle picked up further momentum and slipped down into the clouds.

Shit. Shit. Shit. That bottle was still half-full, and water is absolutely crucial to survive at that altitude. I could see Marvin shaking his head and looking furiously at me. I called out to him, "Hey, don't worry. I've still got another one."

I did indeed have another liter bottle in my pack, but it wasn't the one I thought it would be. Instead of bringing a second bottle of water, I had mistakenly packed the bottle that I pee in at night. Oh my gosh, I was so embarrassed. And Marvin was making things worse, accusing me of doing this on purpose for some reason, although I couldn't figure out why anyone would deliberately jettison a water bottle that was necessary for survival. While Marvin was threatening to send me back down, Lakpa jumped in and offered to share his bottle with me.

Marvin was still furious with me on the way down. "I read your file in the office about your first trip to the Cascades."

I just kept my head down and continued walking, hoping he'd just leave me alone. I felt badly enough as it was.

"It said that prior to that climb you had absolutely no mountaineering experience whatsoever. I have no idea what you think you are doing here on an 8,000-meter climb. It took me fifteen years of training and experience to get to this point. But now you show up and think you can do this after a year. What were you were thinking? Why did they even let you come on this expedition?"

I thought of all the things I could have said in response, but I could feel the tears starting to fall, and I didn't want him to know how much he was hurting me.

"Look," he continued in a scolding tone, "I'm the one in charge of this team. Don't you ever think you can go to Lakpa and that he'll help you. If I say you're done, that's it, you're done. That means you go back down. Do you understand me?"

I nodded.

"I said do you understand?"

I'd had time to regain my composure. My goggles were starting to fog up from the tears, so I lifted them up onto my helmet and turned to face him fully. "Yes, I understand," I told him in a voice that was surprisingly steely and calm. "That's the reason why I'm climbing with you. Because I trust your expertise and experience. And I know you are just concerned about my safety." As I said this, I was smiling, I suppose because I was nervous and upset—and that seemed to just enrage him further.

"See, right now, you're just smiling at me. Like you don't take me seriously."

I tried again. For the life of me, I couldn't figure out why Marvin was so mean and on my case all the time. I told him one more time that I appreciated his help and suggestions, but he still didn't seem to believe me. He just shook his head and walked away, ignoring me all the rest of the way down.

Good Cop, Bad Cop

"He's just always on my back," I was telling Laura, still upset and crying while we were talking in our tent. "What the hell does that even mean, that I smile when he talks to me or that I don't take him seriously?"

Laura was trying to calm me down and take care of me, just like the big sister she had become to me. While I lay on my bag feeling sorry for myself, she helped me take off my boots and climbing gear.

"And *now* what am I going to do with only one bottle for water, plus my pee bottle? I don't even know where my extra bottle is; I thought I left it in the tent." The tears started flowing once again.

We talked for a while longer, and then I knew I had only one option left: I would have to drink out of my pee bottle, which had the most putrid smell of old, fermented urine. I could even see yellowy crust along the bottom that seemed impossible to scrape out through the narrow opening at the top. I tried putting snow inside and rubbing it around, but it didn't seem to help much. I was going to have to drink pee water for the rest of the trip, and that seemed the absolute end of my self-control. My only saving grace, one that would earn us all a respite, was that the Sherpas had more rope fixing to do on the steeper parts ahead of us, which meant we would have to descend back down to Advanced Base Camp.

Once we arrived back at ABC, I tried to regroup. I washed my clothes and tried to disinfect the pungent scent from my pee bottle. The good news was that once we descended back down to 18,000 feet, it felt to me like sea level, compared to where we'd been. I felt strong once again as we started back up to Camp One, followed by another grueling day back on the ice cliff. Whatever optimism I had temporarily entertained was crushed yet again once we got off the wall, and I could barely walk back to camp without falling. Lakpa, who still took a special interest in me, reached into my pack to remove some of the items and put them in his own pack. This time when I cried, it was with such love and appreciation for his incredible caring and support.

I felt like I was being bounced around like a ping-pong ball by the classic good cop, bad cop routine. But I also realized how much more emotionally reactive I'd become at such a high altitude. It was something to remember if I ever tried this again.

A Flood of Tears

After another successful rotation we were back at Advanced Base Camp. Finally, after breakfast, we were told that this would be our last rotation before reaching the summit. We would head back up to Camp One, then on to Camp Two, and then still higher to Camp Three, the last stop before the summit. We were all so excited but also lost in our own thoughts about whether we would make it after so many others had given up.

The going was definitely easier this time heading back up to our Camp One. We were on our way to Camp Two, almost to the ice cliff, when Marvin approached me with his characteristic scowl. "How much water are you carrying?" he asked in a challenging voice.

All I could think to myself was *Don't smile. Don't smile, whatever you do.* I knew I was on solid ground, so I told him I had the regulation two bottles with me.

"Show me," he said, and I was stunned that he didn't believe me. Why on earth would I lie about something like that? Even more curious, why would I deliberately carry only one bottle when I knew it would put my life in danger? Did he actually think that I would do such a thing just to show him he couldn't order me around? It was crazy.

I reached into my pack and pulled out the first bottle, and then the second one, almost defiantly.

"What's this?" he said in a voice so loud that others began gathering around us. He was pointing to my second bottle, which was about three-quarters full.

"What do you mean?" I was totally confused.

"I mean you are a liar."

"Excuse me?"

"You're a liar. You lie about everything."

At this point, there were more than thirty climbers watching this exchange, all of whom had stopped to rest at the same spot. They were all watching this interaction with curiosity.

"Are you serious?" I asked him, absolutely stunned. Just because I had already consumed a little bit of the water from one bottle, he was saying I had lied to him. This was utterly ridiculous. It was my turn to become furious. He was humiliating me in front of my friends and fellow climbers.

"Why do you hate me so much?" I asked.

"What do you mean?" he responded.

"Why do you give me such a hard time? Aren't you supposed to be *helping* me, not breaking me down?" If he thought my smile was disturbing, he must have loved my look of complete contempt.

"That's it," he said. "You're done here. I'm not taking you any further."

Just when I was about to totally lose it and go off on him, he stomped away, leaving me alone. Everyone else who had watched this scene pretended to ignore what happened, but for me, this was the last straw.

I followed Marvin and screamed to his back, "I'm done. I'm tired of your crap."

"Fine," he said with this look of triumph. "Go back down."

"No, I mean *you*. You've been hired to take care of me, to help me, not humiliate me. How dare you speak to me this way, call me a liar, and in front of all these people. You are the worst guide ever!"

At that point, another guide came between us. "Okay guys, calm down. It's okay." Then Marvin gave me a scornful look and walked away.

After that, it seemed like people were avoiding me. Even Laura was nowhere to be seen. Maybe they thought I was infectious. So I walked alone for the next few minutes, tears streaming down my cheeks. With the warmth of the sun reflecting off the snow, there was no risk of my tears freezing, so I just let myself go. When I saw Lakpa walking back toward me, I tried to compose myself. I knew he would say the right thing and comfort me, but this time he surprised me.

"Why are you crying?" he asked. "Crying doesn't fix anything. You must stop crying. You're losing your body's water."

Well, I suppose he was right. But I found that comment absolutely hilarious, and I started laughing like a madwoman. Then, once he left me alone, I started crying all over again.

A Long Night

Once we arrived at Camp Two after another exhausting day, Marvin was high-fiving everyone, saying, "Good job, everyone!" Everyone but me, that is. I went inside my tent to hide, and I dissolved into more tears. A few minutes later, Marvin stuck his head inside, asking me if I wanted to talk about what was going on.

"Sure," I said. "I'm totally open to whatever you want to tell me to improve my skills, but I don't appreciate you scolding me all the time in front of everyone else. If you have something constructive to offer me, I would like you to do it in private. And I also don't like that you called me a liar."

To my utter shock, he immediately apologized. "Look, I'm sorry I did that. From now on, I'm not going to criticize you. I *do* know you've got this. You've already made it to Camp Two, and you are still strong. So I'll do my best to stay out of your way." With that, he ducked outside the tent, leaving me alone once again to my tears. I was dumbfounded by his change of attitude and apology.

Laura tried her best to calm me down. "Climbing this damn mountain is hard enough," she reassured me. "You certainly don't need this additional aggravation. And you can always climb with another company and never see him again." She was referring to the likelihood that he would also be the head guide assigned to my next scheduled Everest expedition.

I wish I could say that this made me feel better, but I was still feeling sorry for myself, and so I cried myself to sleep once again. I just felt so miserable, so misunderstood, and so alone. I had never realized that the hardest part of the climb wouldn't be the mountain itself but rather all the interpersonal undercurrents and dynamics that were involved in reaching the summit. If you've read or seen stories about tragic climbing accidents, so often they involve competitive contests or misunderstandings among members of the team.

I later woke up in the middle of the night and had to pee so badly that I felt like I was going to explode. But it was so frigid outside that there was no way I was going out there. In turned out that another team member had decided to quit the climb, enabling me to inherit one of his extra water bottles. So now I was back to peeing through my funnel into my old faithful one. Unfortunately, my legs felt like rubber from the day's journey, and I could barely support myself above the funnel. Before I knew it, my legs collapsed, knocking over the half-full bottle of accumulated urine, which spread all over my sleeping bag and clothes, including the heavy socks I was supposed to wear the next day. Still worse, because I was so dehydrated—even with my consumption of the prescribed water ration—my urine was brown, with the most disgusting toxic smell. It was as if my body was trying to rid itself of all the accumulated poisons—the collective result of poor diet, inadequate oxygen, and psychological torture.

I just squatted there, staring at the mess, watching Laura sleeping and wondering, *What the hell do I do now?* There was no way I was waking up any of the guides and subjecting myself to more scolding. All I could think to do was put on the piss-soaked socks, hoping they would dry sometime during the night in my similarly soaked sleeping bag. When I compared how miserable that night was to the one I spent on Mount Whitney—that fateful night when I thought I was going to die—it was pretty close to a toss-up.

The next morning, the socks were still damp; I had no choice but to wear them. I certainly wasn't about to tell anyone, even Laura, about my calamity. I just couldn't take any more criticism, and I'd lost hope that I'd get sympathy from anyone.

Summit Attempt

By the time we arrived at Camp Three, I had rediscovered some of my passion and excitement. It was a glorious day, absolutely clear and crisp. In every direction, I could see snowcapped peaks rising above the valley far below. We were on top of the world—as high as I'd ever been, not only in terms of altitude but spiritually and emotionally as well. I felt giddy and pure. I also felt strong, really strong and confident for our summit attempt early in the morning.

All the concerns and frustrations of the previous days just seemed to melt away. Even my socks had eventually dried, although when we resettled in camp for a few hour's rest and I removed my boots to massage my feet, I could smell the wafting aroma of the worst combination of scents imaginable. Even that couldn't dent my elated mood.

We watched the sunset, tried to eat something, and then retreated to our tents to get some rest before our wake-up call around 11:00 p.m. Laura and I were so excited we knew that sleep would be impossible, so we lay quietly next to one another and listened to each other's breathing, which had by then become familiar and soothing.

I must have dozed off for a little while, because before I knew it, I heard the wake-up call telling us to get ready. It was terribly cold, even with my down suit, which is rated at minus forty degrees. Surely it couldn't be *that* cold, I thought. But on this morning, I decided nothing would poison my mood.

Lakpa was the lead guide, and I was positioned right behind him, with Kami, his brother, right behind me. I was sandwiched between two of my favorite Sherpas; once again, it was as if the spirits of the universe had answered my call. Even better, Marvin was the "sweep" guide, all the way at the end of our team and as far away from me as possible. By that point, I couldn't even stand looking at him. Once again, it felt like the gods had answered my prayers.

I could see a long line of lights sparkling in the distance all the way up the mountain. These were other climbing teams that had left before us, hoping to avoid the crowds. We were now using oxygen to assist us, which made things so much easier, but even with the flow adjusted to maximum capacity, we could rely on the assistance for only a limited time, especially with all the climbers ahead of us who might slow us down.

For the first time, we had to do some seriously vertical rock climbing, which, at that altitude, was truly exhausting. Lakpa could see me struggling and called out to me: "This is the hardest part. Once we get through the rocks, the rest will be much easier."

I just nodded, unable to talk intelligibly through the oxygen mask.

Climbing rocks with crampons and heavy boots is quite challenging, the spikes squeaking and scraping along, barely providing any kind of purchase. It felt like any moment I'd lose my grip. I could see Lakpa watching me carefully, and I knew Kami was right behind me, providing some reassurance. I just hoped I didn't fall and take them both down with me, since we were connected by ropes.

There was one team in front of us that was climbing without oxygen, and they were going much slower than our pace. We were all connected to one another by the same guide rope, so that meant that in order to pass them, we had to unclick ourselves, pass around them, and then reattach ourselves. During those few minutes, we were dangerously vulnerable to a fatal fall without a net. One slip and I'd be gone, possibly pulling the others down with me.

After nine hours of steady, relentless climbing, just as we approached the summit, I could see the sun beginning to peek out, and for the first time I could see all the ice and glaciers around us. There were 20,000-foot mountains all along the horizon, but they were dwarfed by Cho Oyu, which is the tallest among them on this side of the border. However, the first thing I noticed when we reached the top was majestic Everest rising still further into the sky; it was so close I thought I could almost leap over there. Next to it was Lhotse, which was almost at eye level with me.

I turned around and saw all the prayer flags flapping in the wind. There is just no way I can possibly describe the feeling of exhilaration from doing something so incredibly difficult, wanting to give up a hundred times yet still forcing myself to endure all the hardships and continuing anyway. One year before, I'd never in my life been in the mountains or even camping, and there I was, standing at 27,000 feet. It was like an out-of-body experience, almost like I was weightless. I felt so, so thankful for the opportunity to experience this, no matter how difficult it had been to get to that point.

There isn't much time to celebrate once you reach the summit of a Himalayan peak. You are standing at the same height as planes flying along the jet stream. It's absolutely freezing, thirty degrees below zero. The wind is blowing at fifty miles an hour. At best, you've got just a few minutes to take in the experience, and then you have to get out of there before it's too late. So I took out the Empower Nepali Girls banner that I'd been carrying with me all that time. I stretched it out between my arms, trying to hold it steady so it wouldn't blow away like the last time I had tried to do that. I asked Lakpa to take a photo for me to show to the girls when I returned to Kathmandu and the villages.

I took out my own camera to capture the moment and the spectacular views. The damn thing was frozen, the battery dead. I had anticipated that possibility, so I'd made sure to keep my phone inside my jacket to keep it warm as a backup. I checked the battery and found it registering 100 percent, but after I'd taken just a few photos, it also died. No matter: I tried to burn those unforgettable images into my brain. I remember reading somewhere that when you take a photo of something, you are actually *less* likely to remember the experience, since your brain somehow knows not to waste memory space holding onto a visual artifact that has been recorded elsewhere. I don't know if that is true or not, but I did often find that taking pictures interrupted the primacy and intensity of a significant experience, so I just gazed around in awe, trying to hold onto those precious moments that I had worked so hard to earn. Truthfully, the whole scene was so improbably spectacular, it seemed like it wasn't real.

The Long Way Down

Once again, we were reminded that often the most dangerous part of a summit climb is on the way down. Only 15 percent of the climbers who died on Everest perished while heading up to the summit; the rest died on the way down or when turning back. People are exhausted and sleep-deprived, having been on their feet already for eighteen hours or longer. The chronic lack of oxygen impairs cognitive processing, so poor decisions are made. Legs feel like they are about to collapse. It's much harder to navigate downward steps when sometimes you can't see where you are placing your feet. And what you *can* see is sometimes terrifying, since the sheer drop-offs hidden during the night are now all too visible. Inevitably, mistakes are made. So we were warned, in spite of our exhilaration at having finally reached our goal, to use caution and care as we descended.

Once we had all safely returned to camp, I tried to rest for a few hours. You'd think that after forty-eight hours with virtually no sleep, I'd fall unconscious immediately, but a few hours later, I was awakened by some foreign spirit that seemed to have entered my body. Once again, my legs were vibrating of their own volition, as if they had a mind of their own. I was shaking so bad it felt like I had absolutely no control. I actually wondered if I was dying, if my body was literally falling apart. I had a racking cough that hurt my chest every time I let loose. My muscles, my joints, and even my internal organs ached for relief. I took painkillers, but they didn't seem to put a dent in the misery, so I just lay in my sleeping bag for hours, hoping the suffering would either stop or kill me. It was the single worst night of my life. I realized then the price I had paid for this experience.

The next morning, all of us tried to engage in a celebratory mood, but most of us could barely walk. Much later, once we descended through Camp One and arrived back at Advanced Base Camp, we were more inclined to enjoy what we'd done. We held a special ceremony to honor and thank our guides and porters, tipping them generously for their courage and support.

We reversed course, passing through the same villages and teahouses we had seen during the beginning of our journey, but everything looked and felt different. *We* were different.

Unfinished Business

After we arrived back in Kathmandu, I was over the moon, excited about my prospects of tackling Everest next. I was a physical wreck and still quite emotionally wounded from the interpersonal drama on the mountain, but I was also feeling more optimistic than ever about continuing my mission.

There was, of course, one significant piece of unfinished business: getting together with Marvin to clear the air, since I was concerned that he might end up as my guide on the summit attempt of Everest. I sure didn't want to get into more conflict with him, especially considering how important it was to keep my head straight and focused on the tasks at hand instead of worrying about how he might continue to needle and shame me.

We met in the hotel lobby, an oasis of luxury after what we'd been through the past few months. There was endless hot water, actual heat in the rooms, and restaurants where I could order anything I wanted.

Marvin and I sat across from one another, and there was definitely an uneasy silence between us. I decided to be as gracious and accommodating as I could with him, not wanting to trigger any additional tension between us.

"So," I began tentatively, "I know we had some difficulties on the mountain. I thought it might be a good idea for us to—"

Marvin kind of waved his hand as if to say it was no big deal. I could see he was really uncomfortable with our situation when I was just trying to normalize things between us.

"Um, I was saying that I really value your help and expertise and the ways you try to support me." Okay, that was a stretch, if not a big fat lie, but as I said, I was just trying to deescalate any further problems between us. I was at a point where I sincerely believed I could handle the physical demands of the next level, but I was more concerned with what had felt like psychological torture. I'm not saying that's what Marvin intended, but that's what it had felt like to me.

Marvin just nodded noncommittally. I suppose he was wondering where I was going with this conversation and perhaps even thinking that I was still really upset and might get him in trouble or something. I needed to reassure him that was not at all what I intended.

"On Cho Oyu, you gave me a number of suggestions to improve my climbing and roping techniques, so I was wondering, as I continue to prepare for Everest, what other recommendations you might have for me." As I said these words, I thought to myself, *And please don't mention one more time those stupid water bottles!*

I could see visible signs of relief on Marvin's face once he realized that I wasn't there to argue with him but rather to try and become friends. We spent a pleasant hour chatting about some of the more amusing events that had transpired during our adventures, after which Marvin turned serious and once again repeated what he had told me toward the end of the climb when he admitted that I was a lot stronger and more resilient than he'd ever given me credit for. He actually said he was quite proud of me. I appreciated his graciousness in admitting he'd been wrong.

It was surprising that we'd actually reached a point in our relationship where Marvin told me he hoped he would be my guide on Everest, which was quite a turnaround. He also made some helpful suggestions about adjustments I could make to some of my equipment, including trying out a smaller backpack that would better fit my smaller frame. We embraced in an awkward hug and promised to stay in touch.

As excited and satisfied as I felt about the successful summit and reveling in my newly acquired identity as a mountaineer, I couldn't stop thinking about the scholarship girls I'd met so briefly. Yes, I was looking forward to my return visit to Nepal in a few more months to attempt Everest, but I was just as eager to spend more time with the children. When I returned in the spring, Jeffrey promised that he would arrange for more opportunities for me to visit schools and homes and to learn more about how the organization operated as well as the background on how things had evolved.

View of Everest

Jeffrey
December 2014–January 2015

Many years ago, I developed a rather unique strategy for both raising money and mentoring the children we support. I was well aware that throwing money at causes hardly makes much of a difference, especially in places where corruption and fraud are so rampant. Something like 90 percent of all charities in Nepal never distribute a single dollar to a cause; they just collect donations and pay themselves salaries and expenses so that there is little money left to distribute.

Our organization was constructed based on a model of complete transparency. Everyone pays their own travel expenses. There were no salaried employees (and not even an office) until the last few years. Because I work with graduate students, many of them have been active in raising funds and traveling with me to Nepal to help mentor the girls.

Sara was excited to join our annual trip to distribute scholarships and visit all the children in the villages. During her previous visit, she had had the chance to meet only a few of the girls in the capital city, and I knew she was eager to meet hundreds of others who lived in more remote regions, not only along the Everest trail but also in far more isolated areas that rarely ever receive visitors.

I was in the process of transferring leadership to a new team that was headed by a former technology executive. I was also interested in persuading Sara to take on a more active leadership role within the foundation because of her commitment and spectacular success raising money for the girls. On this particular trip, we had recruited twenty volunteers who had all been active in fundraising throughout the year. Some of those who were joining us had been involved for many years.

Our new president and his wife were joining the trip along with several other veterans, including a university professor and her family, and a psychiatrist who arrived with her daughter. In addition to these experienced members, I invited along several of my graduate students, all of whom had just completed their first semesters in our counseling program. Each of them made a leap of faith to sign up even though they were already in debt, supporting their studies. It seemed that almost everyone who joined these expeditions made huge sacrifices to do so, not only financially but also by choosing to be away from their loved ones during the holidays.

My wife, Ellen, was joining us as well. She worked as a professor in the same university where I taught, and she specialized in preparing secondary school teachers, so her expertise was especially valuable. She also served as the foundation's bookkeeper and was returning to Nepal for the sixth time. Finally, another tech executive was the last member of our team. In addition, we had a documentary film crew with us who were creating a production to showcase the work that the foundation was doing. The producer was especially interested in our work because she had just completed a feature film about sex trafficking in Nepal called *Brave Girl*.

Because our group was so large, we would divide into smaller units to conduct the home and school visits. It was hardly feasible to show up to a girl's home the size of a small room and file inside with two dozen people. The plan was for us to split in half throughout the visit, sending one group to one region while the others visited another area. Because we had so much territory to cover—more than a dozen villages spread across the country—this would allow us to visit almost every one of the three hundred girls in the program.

Career Conference

One of the challenges we'd faced in the past was that the girls knew very little about the options available to them. They'd rarely ever seen a woman working in a profession. The only jobs they'd seen for women were as teachers or nurses. During the previous years, we'd been trying to inspire them to strive for higher education and other career opportunities. That was one reason why Sara's presence as an engineer, professor, and mountaineer was potentially so inspirational. Also, several of the other women with us were physicians, engineers, and computer specialists, professions that were typically and exclusively dominated by men in that part of the world.

It had been my original dream, fifteen years before, that perhaps someday the girls might become doctors and the next generation of leaders in their country. There were now two girls whom we'd been supporting for many years and who were now in the process of applying for medical school. Unfortunately, because they were from poor families and had no connections with government officials, they were closed out of spots within Nepal, so we were arranging for them to study in Bangladesh. Many of the other children also aspired to careers in medicine, a goal that was likely unrealistic, given the meager financial resources available, not to mention the limited spaces available for women.

This year, our plan was to organize a career conference (as we'd done the prior year) to introduce them to possibilities they hadn't considered. In addition to the women on our team, we invited prominent Nepali professional women to talk to the girls about their own journeys.

We organized the event inside a school, and it was packed with more than 150 of the girls—those from the Kathmandu Valley as well as others from outlying districts whom we had brought into the capital city for the first time. These children lived in isolated rural areas and had never wandered far from their villages, much less ever traveled on a bus before. Also, the day before, we had organized walking tours of all the famous temples and tourist sites so the girls and our volunteers would have the chance to get to know one another. The key to our mentoring program was for our team members to become role models for the girls, to show them what was possible.

Sara talked about her work as an engineer as well as the challenges of being a woman climber. The girls understood how difficult it was to function in a male-dominated culture in which everything seemed so much harder for girls, who were often prohibited from the best education, jobs, and opportunities. They were especially amused hearing Sara describe how some male climbers were disheartened when they encountered a small woman who was so much stronger than they were. You could see their minds working, thinking about ways this was familiar to them.

They were also intrigued by the other women in our group who also held important positions in medicine, academia, industry, and technology. These were positions in Nepal that were almost exclusively limited to men. The girls were just as impressed with the students in our group who were pursuing their own ambitious careers.

Perhaps most impressive of all to them was Babita (our second in command after Pasang), whom we had sponsored to complete her master's degree in social work. Because Pasang is busy so much of the time with his trek-guiding responsibilities and the executive functions of the organization, Babita was now taking charge of the daily operations. And she is the one the girls trust most when they need help. She is truly the perfect image of what we hoped for all the girls.

The reason we had invited Nepali women representing various professions to the conference and encouraged them to speak to the girls about their career trajectories was to highlight many options they may not have considered before. We wanted to expose the girls to jobs that were not only more realistic but also more affordable, given our limited budget and the astronomical costs of sponsoring girls in higher education: it costs several thousand dollars for each girl per year instead of about a hundred dollars for primary and secondary school.

The highlight of the conference was the viewing of a new film, which told the story of a fourteen-year-old Nepali girl who was tricked into leaving her village to find a good job in the city. Like many other such girls, she ended up being sold to a brothel in India. The producer thought it was fitting to screen the world premiere of the movie for the very children she was hoping to help save instead of at one of the major film festivals (that would soon follow).

If you know anything about the typical Bollywood films that are prevalent in South Asia, the basic plot involves a love story (with lots of dancing and music) that *always* has a happy ending. The children gasped as the final scene in *Brave Girl* drew to a close because they'd never seen a film that ends with the protagonist ending up a sex slave, sentenced to die by repeated rape. We had hoped this would scare the heck out of them and show them the importance of being cautious and mistrusting of offers from strange men that sounded too good to be true. The film did its job for sure!

Afterwards, the main actress, who was still in high school herself and the same age as many of our older girls, spoke to the assembly not only about her experience making the film but also about the extent to which Nepali girls were being exploited, forced into early marriage, and sold into slavery. She compiled a remarkable slideshow presentation that was an incredibly powerful experience for all of us.

There were whispers among all the girls who realized that Sara was the woman who would be climbing Everest on their behalf. They wondered how this relatively tiny, gorgeous woman could climb mountains on top of everything else she was doing in her career. It was amazing to them that a woman could be an engineer and professor, but beyond their imagination that she could also be a world class athlete.

But those accomplishments didn't impress them as much as Sara's accessibility did. At any given moment, there were several girls climbing on her lap and another holding on to her neck in one hug-ball of tickles and giggles. Whereas some of our team members were rather reluctant (and, frankly, frightened) by the strange environment with all the chaos around us, that didn't hold Sara back at all. She just dove into the crowd of children, asking them questions, hugging them, and organizing games for them to play together.

"*Mero nam Sara ho*," she said to one group of girls, telling them her name in Nepali, and they loved it, offering other words for her to pronounce: *sahti* (friend), *didi* (older sister), *dai* (older brother). After each repetition, they would carefully correct Sara's accent, absolutely loving the idea they could teach her their language. Then they tested her by telling Sara their names and asking her to go around the circle and repeat each of them in order.

My students observed Sara's interactions curiously and then followed her lead, spreading out among the children to engage them. It was just one huge sisterly gathering; little circles spread around the cavernous room or on the field outside the school, with each of our volunteers engaged in various activities. Babita and several of her friends and social work students circulated among the crowd, providing support as needed.

After the event was completed, all of us returned to Pasang's home to debrief, eat a traditional Nepali dinner of *dal baht*, drink, and dance all night. I was so exhausted and jetlagged that I was on the verge of passing out, but Sara was out there dancing with all the other young women, imitating their traditional moves and teaching them a few of her own. I had no idea where she had gotten that kind of energy, but it was obvious she had recovered physically from her last climb.

A Grand Time

After spending a week visiting with many of our children from the southern districts as well as those within the Kathmandu Valley, we split our team in half to visit the girls who live deep in the Everest and Annapurna Himalayan regions. Although I'd flown to Lukla (the gateway to Sherpa culture) a half dozen times, this would be Sara's first trip to finally see where she and her climbing team would be arriving a few months later. It was kind of an advanced scouting mission for her as well as an opportunity to learn more about the organization.

It's remarkable to land a small plane on such a remote strip—sandwiched between high mountains in all directions—disembark, and then begin walking in one of the most beautiful places in the world. The flight is one of the most spectacular (and dangerous) in the world, since the plane has to thread between two mountains, make a tight left turn, and then land on a very short, upwardly angled runway that abruptly ends on the slope of another mountain.

After fortifying ourselves with cappuccinos at the "fake" Starbucks (complete with a counterfeit green sign), our first stop was to visit the local school that several of the children attended. They had organized a ceremony and dance for us to celebrate the scholarship awards. As we sat together on the school's grounds overlooking the Everest trail, we could see teams of climbers and trekkers passing by below us, so lost in their determination to reach Base Camp that they were oblivious to the people whose lives they were passing by.

Normally, it would just be a two-hour walk to our lodge for the evening, but with frequent stops along the way to visit the girls in their homes or talk to them along the trail, it took most of the day. Pasang had called ahead, so everywhere we walked, children literally appeared out of nowhere to greet us, welcome us, and follow us along on our journey.

The next day, prior to beginning our work, we took off for an acclimatization hike to help us adjust to altitude because eventually, we would be going above 17,000 feet on this trip. This was perhaps not very high by Sara's standards, but for the rest of the group, it was a lofty goal. At dawn, we started up the mountain, following a steep, narrow yak trail that weaved in and out through the forest until we reached a plateau with gorgeous views of the valley below. Everyone but Sara was exhausted and wanted to turn back, so we headed down, knowing that a bunch of the girls were waiting for us at the lodge.

The children in this area tend to be extremely shy, and the quality of the education is so poor that their English is sometimes a struggle to understand. The schools typically consist of stone buildings that might hold a handful of small rooms crowded with ancient wooden desks. Considering that it is absolutely freezing during winter months at this altitude (above 10,000 feet) and some of the children don't have shoes, much less warm clothes, classes were cancelled until things warmed up in the early spring.

We often organized our own impromptu classes for the children, helping them to practice their English and reviewing their math homework. I think what was also most appreciated is that we fed them, because many of girls look like they've not had a good meal in a long time. While I was observing the interactions among our team members and several girls using iPads (which they'd never seen before) to learn vocabulary, I heard screaming outside. I looked out the window to see Sara standing in the middle of a circle of about twenty girls. I wasn't sure what the rules of this game were all about, but by the sounds of their laughing and screams, they were all having a grand time.

Located high up on a ridge overlooking the river valley below was another school that served children who were still more isolated. There were steep cliffs upon which their homes seemed to balance precariously. I remember that one of our scholarship girls and her family died the previous year when a mudslide washed them away. She was an adorable little girl who I once held on my lap, and it still saddens me to think about her.

Each school we visited had its own special ceremony to honor us as important foreign visitors. In one particular place, we watched hundreds of children doing their morning warmup exercises. This was followed by dancing, which was joined by several among our group, moving gracefully as they lined up behind the children. Then Sara got up in front to demonstrate Persian dances, which absolutely delighted the children, who followed every step and move.

Breakfast with Everest

We continued onward and upward through villages, sometimes following the standard trekking route but more often than not following yak trails along the ridges where many of the children lived, way off the beaten trail. During each home visit, we would be offered tea or sometimes little boiled potatoes (about all that they could harvest and store that time of year). We would sit and visit for several minutes and then ask each girl to show us her schoolwork. Before leaving and moving on to the next place, we would take turns speaking to the parents and urging them to support their girl's study. It was exhausting and emotionally draining, seeing how these people lived with so few resources and even the most basic necessities. There were times when I would hear their stories of hardship and deprivation and I could barely hold in my own anguish before I would walk outside and start sobbing uncontrollably.

We completed our last school and home visits and now had a full week to do some trekking in this beautiful area. This was intended as both a reward and as sacred reflective time to metabolize all we'd seen and done. It was also useful for us to process everything together, debrief about what seemed to work best, and make future plans for what needed to be done next. It was Pasang's idea, for instance, that some of the more talented girls might be brought to Kathmandu in order to receive a better education. There was one girl, only ten years old, who had performed a dance recital for us and was so remarkably talented that she had already placed second in the nation for her age group. We thought it might be a good idea to hire a professional choreographer for her to further improve her performances, since this might become a viable career. She'd already been invited to Korea for a performance.

The next few days were so wonderfully relaxing—and vigorous. This was nothing like Sara's summit attempts, but it was still pretty challenging terrain as we moved up higher and higher and the weather got colder and colder. We were headed toward Namche Bazaar, the capital of the Sherpa region, but rather than going into the village itself (which I'd done several times previously), our goal was a lodge perched high on a 15,000-foot mountain that overlooked the village below. This would be the highest altitude at which most of us had ever slept.

The next day, we climbed a mountain topping off at over 17,000 feet. It took most of the day because of the deep snow that was up to our thighs. By the time we returned to the lodge, everyone immediately headed to bed—everyone except Sara, who decided she wanted to do the climb a second time; after all, she was now training for Everest.

The morning of our departure, breakfast was set out for us in the most elegant setting imaginable. There was a dining table and chairs, each emblazoned with ribbons and bows and positioned toward Mount Everest, rising in the distance. This was the best view Sara had yet of her next destination. With complete reverence, we watched the sun rise above the Himalayas, bathing the majestic mountain in pink light. Afterwards, we would begin the long, arduous walk back down the mountain, through all the villages, past all the girls standing along the trail, to the airport in Lukla, to Kathmandu, and then home. We never imagined that everything in this area of the country, in this region of the world—particularly where we were sitting—would be leveled by the earthquakes that would soon follow.

Finally Ready for Everest

Sara
February–March 2015

As I was beginning my final preparations and training for my third trip to Nepal, I couldn't help but draw even more motivation and strength from my memories of the children that continued to haunt me. I remembered visiting one particular classroom in which I asked the girls to come up to the front so I could test them on their favorite subjects. If they'd say math, then I'd write a quadratic equation on the board and ask them to solve it, thinking there'd be no way they'd have such an advanced grasp of these concepts. And if they'd mention science, then I'd pose a difficult question about biology or chemistry. But what shocked me most was that even with their minimal resources, no equipment, and only a few books to share, these girls were absolutely brilliant.

I recall visiting one girl's home so she could show me her homework. This was a wooden and stone hut, hobbled together with mud. While I sat on a straw stool by the fire and sipped chai tea, Priti went into the back to retrieve a notebook. I noticed that half the pages were devoted to chemistry and the other half to English grammar. "Why are you using one notebook for both subjects?" I asked her.

Priti kind of shrugged. "I only have this one notebook."

When I heard that, I could feel tears beginning to form, and I realized I was not only crying for this smart girl who wanted so badly to do well in school; I was also crying for myself when I remembered that I, too, couldn't afford notebooks when I started university at UCLA—until that magical truck came by.

I pretended the smoke was making my eyes water and wiped them with my sleeve. "So," I said in a shaky voice, "show me what you are doing in science," and she proceeded to turn the pages and point out what she'd been learning.

"Okay," I said after a long pause, "if you mix sulfuric acid with calcium, write out the equation for me to show the result."

Priti broke out in a huge grin, not at all shy any longer, and immediately wrote it out.

"Wow," I said, genuinely impressed. "So, what do you intend to do with all this science?"

She mumbled something, retreating back into shyness once again.

"What's that you said? Speak up!"

"I said a doctor. I want to be a doctor." She was almost embarrassed to say this out loud because it seemed like such a ridiculous fantasy.

"Good for you!" I said, grabbing her shoulders and giving her an affectionate hug. "You are so, so smart. You can do this! And I can help you." In that moment, I felt I would not only climb Everest—I'd be willing to climb all the way to the moon so that Priti, and the other girls like her, could pursue their dreams.

Training Flashbacks

In order to take things to the next level of my training, I once again hired a coach who specialized in preparing elite athletes and mountaineers. The first thing Tim told me was that most of the work we'd be doing together would be inside my head rather than merely strengthening my muscles and conditioning my endurance. He warned me that he would push me so far beyond my limits that I would no longer be certain how far I could really go. After all, so much of climbing is mental stamina, being able to tolerate discomfort and suffering. This training would improve my performance not only on the mountain but also in all other aspects of my life.

I knew exactly what Tim meant because based on the experiences I'd already had in the mountains, plus my stay at the silent meditation retreat, I realized I was a very different person than I used to be. I was so much more tolerant and patient. I also felt like there was almost nothing that was beyond my reach. After all, if someone like me, with no experience, no previous training—or even exposure—to climbing, could scale some of the highest peaks in the world, surely almost anything else was possible. These were the kinds of thoughts I repeated to myself over and over when Tim devised new and ingenious ways to push me beyond my limits during our daily sessions. This encouraged me to consider other goals that had been circulating in my head. If I managed to climb Everest, could I continue on and try the rest of the Seven Summits, the highest mountains on each continent? Could I even pursue a PhD, now that I was becoming increasingly interested in leadership and advocacy? Nothing seemed out of bounds.

Pretty early in our program, Tim greeted me at the gym with a grin on his face that he could barely restrain. "I've got a special treat for you today."

"Oh yeah?" I answered with some trepidation, wondering what he could possibly have dreamed up next after we had already run through the usual assortment of boot camp exercises. He seemed to take delight in pushing me to the point of collapse.

"Voila!" Tim said, pointing over his shoulder at a contraption that looked like a medieval torture device. It was actually a sled attached to long ropes, and it had weights on it.

I looked at it quizzically, and he explained with a laugh that this was my new "friend."

Tim connected me to the device, sat on the sideline with a bottle of vitamin water, and proceeded to scream at me to pull the thing back and forth across the room. Every time I lagged a little, he would rise up and follow me, yelling at me to go faster.

Sweat was dripping down my back. I could barely catch a breath. This was insane. This was just out of control. I couldn't do this. I knew that I was supposed to stay focused on the task at hand and not try to run away from the pain in my head; instead, I had to stay with it. It had been explained to me that one thing that separates world-class athletes from amateurs or underachieving pros is that the best among them stay with their suffering rather than try to escape from it. Instead of lapsing into fantasy, distracting themselves with music or podcasts, or trying to anesthetize the pain, really great athletes embrace their suffering. They concentrate even harder on their breathing, their foot placement, their technique. They use the pain as valuable input regarding how far, and how hard, they can push themselves without falling apart.

Nevertheless, I found continued solace and comfort during my brutal training sessions by thinking about the girls I was doing all of this for. I had the most vivid flashbacks and intense floods of memories at unpredictable times. All of a sudden, I could remember being back in Nepal; the sled I was pulling or the wall I was climbing would just disappear, and I would feel this perfect sense of calmness.

On this particular day, when I was first introduced to the sled, it was like I went into a trance, and I was transported back to one teahouse we visited where a few dozen of the scholarship girls were assembled. We started dancing with the girls. The little ones were so light that I could hold both at the same time and dance with them, pick them up, put them down. I tried to remember games from my own childhood that we could play together, but they insisted they wanted to teach me and Jeffrey one of their favorite activities, which they called "Cat and Rat." They invited Jeffrey and me into the center of a huge circle with all the girls holding hands around us. They blindfolded each of us and explained that I would be the rat. I was supposed to make a rat-like sound—"Chee chee, chee chee"—and Jeffrey was supposed to try and catch me, signaling his whereabouts by calling out, "Meow meow." Of course we were both blind, so it was pretty hilarious for the kids to watch Jeffrey trying to catch me. Apparently, he was doing all kinds of crazy things—slithering on the ground, exaggerating his movements with feline grace—all while the children were screaming their heads off.

I was jolted back to the present when I heard Tim speaking to me in a soft voice I could barely hear because I had tuned him out while I was lost in the past. "That's enough," he repeated, telling me it was time for a well-deserved rest.

This was to be my routine for the next few months: going to the gym during the day, running up and down mountains at night, taking care of all the hundreds of details to replace some equipment, and putting my life in order for the months I would once again be gone.

Final Departure

After all these months, even years, of planning, the time had finally come for me to say farewell and begin the final steps of this journey. My sister drove me to the airport, and the one thing we didn't speak about was the very real possibility that I would never be coming home again.

All the climbers I'd ever talked to about this agreed that harm would never happen to them—they were too well prepared and would never make a stupid mistake or go beyond their limits. Denial and dissociation go a long way toward managing such fears. Still, in the back of my mind, I wondered if I was saying goodbye to my family for the last time.

As I was packing my gear and making final arrangements, I started to have second thoughts. It always struck me as more than a little crazy that people would risk their lives for something as stupid as just climbing a mountain. Who would do such a thing, and why? What was missing in their lives that they felt the need to test themselves in such a way? And yet now I was one of those crazy climbers, spending a fortune in expenses, training like a madwoman, leaving all my loved ones behind, jeopardizing my safety and my life—all to subject myself to months of misery living in a tent in one of the most hostile environments in the world. I couldn't help but ask myself what this was really about, beyond helping the children in Nepal. Was there something I was hiding from? Would this finally earn my father's recognition and approval? Would I gain the respect and recognition that I seemed to so desperately desire?

I had no answers, only more questions. And for now, I had to put them aside because it was time to leave.

All my friends and family had surprised me by showing up at the airport to wish me a safe journey. They were wearing tee shirts emblazoned with my photo and the words, "Go, Sara, you can do it!" They had made signs displaying their love and support. My best friend, Pari, handed me a letter she had written. "There's going to be a time on that mountain when you lose hope," she said, "when you want to give up or surrender, when you question yourself and why you are doing this. Read this when you need to be stronger." Then we embraced, and we both started crying.

So many others solemnly gave me bon voyage gifts: a stuffed animal, a bag of dried fruit, a warm scarf, a few lemons (my favorite food). My friend, Mo, handed me a bag of In-N-Out burgers, which are something of a cult favorite in this part of the country. "I know you're gonna miss these for sure," he said.

Once settled on the plane, I checked for messages one last time and found my inbox stuffed with good tidings. There was an email from Jeffrey saying, "You are the strongest person that I know." It meant a lot to me, knowing how strong he is himself and how many people he knows in the world. I had emails from my neighbors and my childhood friends as well as several people I hadn't heard from in years, and I wondered how they even knew about what I was doing. I was overwhelmed with this much love, and I started to feel terribly guilty because I knew there was a chance that I was putting not only my own life in jeopardy but also the welfare of so many others who would also suffer as a result. My constant reassurance was the reminder that this trip wasn't about me at all; it was for the girls.

Once the plane took off, I just stared out the window for hours, wondering if this was the last time I'd ever see the Pacific Ocean. I was trying to be realistic: no matter how careful I was on the mountain, there were so many things that could go wrong that were out of my control—the weather, unstable ice, an unmarked crevasse, a mistake by a climber in front of me. Of course, it never occurred to me that an earthquake could be a factor, especially one that would bring the whole mountain down on top of us.

Blessings

When I arrived at the hotel in Kathmandu, I immediately recognized many of our Sherpas from Cho Oyu, including Lakpa, hanging out in the lobby. It was interesting, though, that they didn't recognize me! I had cut off most of my hair, thinking it would make things so much easier for me on the mountain, since I had so few opportunities to wash it. Even the simplest things we take for granted back home become frustratingly impossible tasks: having to boil water just to brush your teeth, washing yourself with wet wipes without freezing to death, and most frustrating of all for me, just being able to locate the proper garment when you absolutely need it most.

As I approached the group, I could finally see some looks of recognition, first from Lakpa and then from Eric, our lead guide. I was pretty damn excited that Eric would be in charge of our team. He was one of the most experienced and accomplished climbers anywhere, having summited Kilimanjaro sixty-five times, Denali thirteen times, and many of the Himalayan peaks. But just as important to me, he was kind, patient, and accessible. I'd have no fear whatsoever that he would ever publicly (or even privately) humiliate me. In addition to Eric and Lakpa, we'd have Damian with us, an Argentinian who had summited Everest five times. This was an all-star team that included some of the best and most accomplished guides in the world. This definitely increased the probability that we would make it to the summit.

I had arrived before any of the others on our team because I wanted to have some time to visit with the girls and see Babita, Pasang, and his family. I asked Eric to check my gear for me to make sure everything was in order, and then I took off for the day with Babita, who picked me up on her motor scooter, so we could hang out at Pasang's house. They had prepared a special Nepali dinner for me with *momos* (dumplings), *dal baht* (rice and lentils), and for dessert, a cake with "Good luck, Sara" written in icing on the top. Then all the girls from the area started streaming in to show their respect and appreciation, offering me gifts, notes, and cards. The littlest girls had drawn pictures for me, and they all insisted I take their messages with me on the mountain. The girls presented me with flowers and placed *khatas* (silk scarves blessed by the Dalai Lama) around my neck.

I had never felt as blessed as I did in that moment. All these people and children showed up to honor and thank me for what I was doing on their behalf. They held a celebration in my honor, and we all danced together, singing songs and holding hands. There were never fewer than three little girls squirming on my lap at any one time. It was just a magical evening, but I was so totally wasted from lack of sleep and jet lag that I was ready to go back to the hotel and meet the rest of my team.

Just as I was getting ready to leave, an older lady approached me. She was tiny—rail thin—and appeared even smaller because she was hunched over and could barely shuffle along. She reached out her hands to hold my own and started talking to me in Nepali in a soft voice. I could barely hear her, much less understand the words. Babita came over to help translate.

"I am grandmother," the woman said to introduce herself to me.

"Namaskar," I replied, bowing and holding my hands level with my face rather than below my chin to show respect for an elder. With someone older, it is the custom to show even more respect by holding one's hands higher and using the honorific form of "namaste."

"She is my granddaughter," the woman said, pointing to one of the girls I'd been dancing with.

"Yes, she's beautiful."

"She does not have parents. I am the only one."

I just nodded, not sure if that meant she was an orphan or that her parents had died or perhaps even abandoned the little girl.

"I am sick," the woman said. "I have the cancer. I will not live much longer."

I looked toward Babita, who was translating the conversation. I wasn't sure what to say or do. This was just breaking my heart.

"Can you help us?" the woman asked me. "Can you help my granddaughter stay in school after I'm gone? Can you find others to care for her? She's very smart. And she likes to go to school. But now, I don't know what will happen to her when I'm not here."

What else could I possibly say to this woman except that of course I would help her granddaughter? I'd already heard so many stories like this about so many of the girls, and each one inspired me to redouble my efforts to help them. By gosh, I was going to get to the top of Everest if it killed me!

Meet the Team

By the time I returned to the hotel that evening, the rest of our team members had arrived and were getting settled. Orion was a banker by profession, a very tall guy I immediately felt a connection with because of his warmth and kindness. Steve, who was from Canada, was also in the banking business and shared a lot of values and interests with me. He had been supporting children in Afghanistan for many years and was the one who was most interested in the work we were doing with girls in Nepal. Then there was Jon from Australia, a very gregarious, charming, and friendly fellow who turned out to be one of my absolute favorites. Because he was also an electrical engineer by training, we had a lot in common and would spend a lot of time deep in conversation during our journey. "Aussie Jon" had tried climbing Everest the previous year but had been turned back because of the avalanches that had killed so many people. The same thing had happened with Tom, a lawyer from Portland who was back to try again this year. The final member of our team, Kate (who would be my tentmate), brought her eleven-year-old son, Sean, along with a tutor to keep the schoolwork going while they waited at Base Camp when we were up in the mountains. I found it pretty remarkable that an eleven-year-old Western kid could manage to hike up and down the steep mountains we would navigate on the Everest trail, which is pretty grueling in places and considered one of the most challenging treks in the world.

I couldn't possibly have been any happier with our team, our leader, and our Sherpas. Everyone was so friendly and supportive: no big egos or overly demanding, entitled people, which surprised me, considering how prominent and wealthy most Everest climbers tend to be. Sufficiently reassured after meeting everyone, I took my leave once again to return to the Rising Rays School, which I had visited during my last trip to Nepal. There was the usual lineup of children waiting to greet me with flowers and *khatas*. They had made a big sign wishing me luck on the expedition.

All the children crowded around me, peppering me with questions about the upcoming climb. They wanted to know how I trained for Everest and what it was like for a woman to do what men usually do. They wanted to know what I would eat on the mountain, whether I'd be using supplemental oxygen, and most of all, how my family felt about me being gone so long.

The school principal posed a few interesting questions himself about our plans for reaching the summit. I patiently answered each and every question because I wanted them to understand just how difficult and dangerous this journey would be—what was at stake, not only for me but for them as well. I wanted them to know the hardships I would be facing. Then I had leverage to ask them to promise that their role in this partnership would be to continue to study hard and do their best in school.

The next day, we flew back to Lukla and continued on to Phakding, the village just a few hours away where many of the girls live. Pasang had alerted the children that I'd be coming through there with our expedition, so I wasn't surprised to see the children waiting for us along the side of the trail. Over the years, they must have seen thousands of trekkers and climbers walk by them as if they were just an invisible part of the scenery, but this time they knew they were waiting for a friend and guest who had promised to return to them, who had promised to support them.

I collected about thirty of the girls who had turned up and escorted them all back to the teahouse where we were staying so I could introduce them to my friends and climbing partners. Each one of the girls introduced herself, then proceeded to offer a *khata* to each of us, wishing us safe passage. Then the usual dancing and games began. This time it included Steve, Aussie Jon, Orion, Tom, Kate, Sean, and all the Sherpas. As many times as they'd been to this part of the world, they'd never seen or experienced anything quite like this—all the incredible energy in the room and all the children's dreams that hung in the balance, dependent on whether support for them would continue. Many of these people have since become our most loyal and dependable donors and are now among my closest friends.

We could only remain there for one night before we had to continue onward, so we hugged the girls to say goodbye. Many of them had walked three hours to greet us and now had to turn around and head back home before dark. We would continue up the trail during the next few days, and all along the way, I would see some of the girls waving in their bright red puffy jackets, sometimes coming down the ridge to say hello and wish us good fortune.

They were long, difficult days on the trail to Base Camp, especially since we stopped a few times along the way to do some acclimatizing hikes. We were still getting used to one another's pace, learning about one another, and trading stories about previous mishaps or adventures. Aussie Jon was pretty hilarious most of the time. He was a master of card tricks and would show them to me any time he sensed I was feeling a little discouraged. He was such a joyful fellow, always telling jokes and kidding around. We confided all kinds of things along the trail, and he talked a lot about how devoted he was to his wife and his three sons.

"Aren't they worried about you and what we're doing up here?" I asked him.

He just shrugged and then proceeded to confess to me that one of his greatest passions was collecting calculators. He said he intended to open a museum someday to display them. I could never tell if he was kidding or not.

The other guys were incredibly nice and supportive as well, but I found myself gravitating to Kate and her son, Sean, the most. I was fascinated by the way that Kate managed to pursue her interests at the same time she was such a devoted mother. I so envied the relationship that she and Sean had and wondered if I'd be able to do that with my own son or daughter someday.

I'd been thinking about this very idea when Damian walked up next to me and scrutinized me with a searching look. I must have appeared lost in concentration or worried, because he placed a hand on my arm to stop me for a moment. "I know you had some difficulties on Cho Oyu," he said. I think he was referring to the fact that I'm so much smaller than everyone else. "But you have a very strong mind. And that is more important than the body. If you listen to us, if you follow our directions and do the things we tell you, I think you can get to the summit of the highest place in the world."

Base Camp and Beyond

Sara
April 2015

After a couple of days walking along the trail, we arrived in Namche Bazaar. It is a rather large village for this remote region, a trading and commercial center for both climbers and trekkers on their way to Base Camp as well as local people who show up for the weekly markets. It is situated in a spectacular valley surrounded by snow-covered Himalayan peaks and stocked with any supplies, treats, or luxuries that one could want. There are not only businesses with climbing equipment and supplies but also bakeries and coffee shops.

As we entered the valley and began the steep climb up to the lodge where we'd be staying, I was walking alongside Aussie Jon, who was always plying me with interesting questions about my life and work. He had been asking me about how to better encourage girls and women to go into engineering, a challenge not only in Nepal but also elsewhere in the world. Almost all of my technical students back home were men. As an engineer himself, he understood that the profession is usually associated with building cars, planes, robots, and missiles (traditionally male-dominated interests), but women tend to be focused on solving different problems, ones related to health and well-being. Then Kate joined the conversation, and we ended up talking about ways to mentor the next generation, which is a subject I found endlessly fascinating.

Conversations

From Namche, our next stop was Tengboche, a World Heritage site and the location of a monastery situated on top of a mountain with a hundred monks living there. Jeffrey had told me stories about his prior visits there, how it was possible to sit with the monks and chant during their meditation ritual. Since we had an extra acclimatizing day for recovery, we had scheduled an audience with the lama, the head monk, in order to bless our journey.

I was intrigued by the German bakery that was next door so I could load up on treats to vary my diet. You can't imagine how bizarre this was: we were literally standing on top of a mountain with views of Everest in the distance. Besides a few teahouses and the monastery, the area is absolutely isolated from the rest of the world, yet there's actually a place that bakes and serves fresh croissants, muffins, and brownies.

The trail we'd been on constantly descends down to the glacial river, crossing rickety bridges suspended over the gorge and then climbing all the way back up to continue along the path. The bridges were sometimes made of wood, often missing slats, which afforded a terrifying view below of the raging river. They were covered in tattered, colorful prayer flags blowing in the wind, the whole structure swaying back and forth. At times a whole train of yaks carrying supplies would start to cross one end while we had just started at the other end, so we'd have to back up and wait our turn. This was peak season, so the delays felt interminable.

All along the trek to Base Camp, from one village to the next, climbing higher and higher, we met and talked with other climbers along the way. On subsequent visits during this time of year I've encountered remarkable individuals on the way to Base Camp, including a man with two artificial legs who summitted Everest, as well as another 80 year old Japanese guy who had done so a few years earlier. One of the most intriguing parts of these trips is not just the climbing but also the opportunities to get to know such interesting people who attempt such adventures. Everyone has a great story to tell about why they are doing this or what they do back in the world. I had been walking with Eric, our lead guide, for the previous hour as we were approaching the last stop before arriving at Base Camp. We had topped off at 17,000 feet at that point, so it helped to keep conversations going between deep breathing.

At one point, I asked him, "How does your wife handle you being gone so much of the time?" I had been thinking about my husband and how often during the last years we'd been separated because of my climbs on Cho Oyu, Rainier, Aconcagua, and other mountains. I figured I had been gone more than six months during the past two years, and there was no doubt it was putting a strain on our relationship. Increasingly, I wondered if he was feeling resentful during the times he lashed out at me or spent so much time traveling on his own. I kept wondering how others handled this challenge, as I wanted to learn how to deal with this since things seemed to be getting worse.

Eric shrugged. "It really is hard on relationships," he admitted. "A lot of people can't handle it, I suppose. That's why so many climbers end up single."

I recognized immediately what he was saying. The divorce rate for mountaineers is something like double that for the general population. It's not just because they are away from home so much of the year; there is definitely a selfish edge to the endeavor, one that often leaves little balance in other aspects of life, including friendships with nonclimbers and relationships with family. There is also another factor in play in that climbers are among the most extraordinarily fit athletes in the world whereas their partners may not share similar devotion to health, creating differences in values and priorities.

Eric was a pretty wise fellow who had obviously given these questions considerable thought and had likely talked about this with a lot of other climbers. All he could offer, however, was that he was lucky to have a partner who understood what he was doing. I had always thought that was the case in my marriage but now I was beginning to question that.

That conversation, and others, seemed to invade my chaotic thoughts during fitful sleep. I've mentioned how difficult it is to rest at high altitude, but during those rare times when I did lose consciousness, I had the most intense, disturbing dreams. They were so vivid they were almost like hallucinations; sometimes I couldn't tell if they were real or not. I had one particularly powerful dream the night before we arrived at Base Camp: I believed all the members of our team spoke fluent Farsi. When I greeted everyone at breakfast the next morning, I started speaking to them in my native language until I realized that they couldn't understand me and thought I'd lost my mind.

That day, we headed up, up, up to Lobuche, the site of a memorial to all the climbers who died on Everest. There was a huge brass plaque embedded in the rocks. It read, "May he have accomplished his dreams."

I wandered through the graveyard of rock monuments, stopping at times to consider the lives of those who had perished. I was surprised that Rob Hall had such a startling simple and modest monument considering his fame and achievements. His fateful expedition had been popularized in both Jon Krakhauer's book, *Into Thin Air*, as well as the movie, *Everest*. The New Zealand guide had been among the most experienced and elite guides in the world, having summitted Everest five times previously. If you remember the story, he chose to remain with one of his clients in the Death Zone who was in critical condition, rather than leave him to save himself. In one of the most heart wrenching moments he called his wife to say goodbye, telling her, "Sleep well my sweetheart. Please don't worry too much."

I just stood there staring at his marker, tears in my eyes. I thought to myself if someone who was that accomplished couldn't make it back what chance did I have? I turned around and considered that all of the hundreds of climbers whose memories were entombed here had once passed this very spot on their way to the mountain. They all believed they were invulnerable and would cheat the odds. Was it arrogance or ignorance that led me to believe that I would escape their fate?

I wandered back to the entrance of the graveyard. As I read the inscription once again, I shook my head, thinking that, first of all, I didn't think dying was part of the dreams they hoped to accomplish. Secondly, I noted the masculine "he" as a reminder that, besides me and Kate, there were not many other women climbers who we'd yet seen.

I felt this incredible pressure to show everyone, especially the men, that I could keep up with them. During these last few days, it had felt like I was an actor on a stage, pretending to be strong, relaxed, and fit. The truth was that I had an excruciating headache, felt dehydrated no matter how much water I drank, and had absolutely no appetite. I just stood in front of this spiritual site and wondered, given how uncomfortable I already felt, whether I would end up being a part of this memorial. These morbid thoughts were interrupted by a wet tongue licking my hand. I looked down to find our new friend and dog companion, who had been following us for the past week and was now our good luck charm. We had named him Khumbu after the icefall we could see looming in the distance.

I rolled my shoulders and tried to stretch out my back, which was stiff from carrying my big backpack. I felt like a mess already, and we hadn't even gotten close to the really hard part. So far, we hadn't even done much climbing at all during our acclimatizing hikes, just mostly going up and down to get used the thin air and cold. That was about to change and become a lot more challenging.

Base Camp

Whatever excitement I felt about finally arriving in Gorak Shep, only a few hours from the Base Camp was tempered by the blizzard-like conditions outside. Even though we were staying in a teahouse, the very last permanent physical outpost in this part of the world, it had been so cold during the night that I had slept with all my clothes on inside my sleeping bag, with a hot water bottle underneath my back. It had been a brutal night, as I could hear everyone snoring and moving around. We were once again above 17,000 feet and it was simply difficult to catch one's breath.

We got a late start the next morning, so we ended up following other climbing teams as well as long lines of yaks carrying supplies. It was like a parade slowly making its way through the soft snow that was quickly accumulating on the trail. I was concentrating so hard on my foot placements that I was startled to feel something hit my back. I looked over my shoulder to see another group of climbers behind me, grinning and pointing at one another to blame whoever had thrown the snowball. I couldn't just ignore this overture, so I hurried around the next turn in the trail to prepare an ambush. With the poor visibility, hiding was pretty easy, and I had my revenge. In fact, a whole battle ensued among more than a dozen of us—launching our missiles, giggling, running around like crazy. For the first time in a while, I finally felt warm.

Once we arrived at Base Camp, I was shocked at how big the place was. It was like a tent city, with hundreds of brightly colored structures that housed the headquarters and sleeping quarters for the dozens of teams that were hoping to summit Everest. What surprised me most, however, was how many people I already knew who were there, climbers I'd not only met along the trail but also those I had encountered during previous expeditions in the Andes, Cascades, and Himalayas.

I was also pleased to see that we wouldn't exactly be deprived of many comforts and luxuries while settled at Base Camp. Our guides and porters had been sent ahead to erect a large tent that would serve as our headquarters and dining room. In addition, we had set up our own tents like a wagon train circle. There was a party atmosphere everywhere; reggae music blared, competing with Nepali songs and rock standards. Hundreds of climbers were going about their business, organizing their equipment, lounging around, making phone calls or sending messages back home, and some leaving or returning from training climbs.

Meanwhile, the snow was falling and was expected to continue for the next week, which was not good news at all for our prospects, since there would be greater danger of avalanches, hidden crevasses, deep snow, and unstable conditions. The "ice fall doctors," Sherpas who are responsible for setting up the ropes and installing the ladders across crevasses and up ice walls, were out in the snowstorm working their magic. We were told it would be a few more days before their work would be completed.

My own tent was easy to find because I had attached an Empower Nepali Girls banner to the side, the same one I intended to carry with me up to the very top of the world. This became a beacon for others to approach me and ask about our organization and what we were doing. Before long, it was like the charity's headquarters, with people asking how they could donate or support our cause. As I've mentioned, many of the climbers were wealthy and privileged (Who else could afford to do this?), so perhaps they felt their own guilt about investing so much time, money, and energy for the sole purpose of transporting themselves to the top of a mountain. It was quite a fertile environment for me to spread the word about our mission, especially considering that the climbers had been seeing the girls, or many just like them, all along their journeys.

There is always a settling in and adjustment to each of our temporary homes. Since we'd be staying in these tents, on and off, for the next two months, it was even more important to get everything organized properly. Although we only bring the stuff we can carry on our own backs and that can fit into a single duffel bag carried by a porter, it still drives me crazy to search for a pair of liner gloves, extra socks, or pen and paper when everything is scattered about. So the first thing I usually do is try to consoidate my equipment so I can find the things that are a priority. This time, however, I was sopping wet through and through from the blizzard and snowball fight, and I could feel the shivers start to take hold. I was also so tired I could barely open my duffel bag.

I was just going to drag out my sleeping bag and try to get some rest when I heard a helicopter land nearby. I poked my head outside to see what was going on and learned that Sean, Kate's son, was being transported back to Kathmandu because the climbing part of our expedition was about to begin.

At that point, sleep was out of the question, so I decided to have a look around my new village, which struck me as a pretty wild and crazy place with lots of interesting characters. The first thing I learned was that we actually had Internet access in this remote place, which seemed crazy to me but certainly welcome. I was able to communicate with people back home and tell them that I was in fine spirits and perfect health. Okay, so I lied a little.

There was actually a complete hospital set up in the camp, so I walked by to check it out and found it fully stocked with medicine, equipment, and qualified physicians who specialized in high-altitude medicine. I asked a few questions while I was there, and the staff reassured me that my own symptoms were perfectly normal and would eventually dissipate once I fully acclimatized. Of course, every time we went higher, my body would have to adapt all over again, at least until we reached a height where the body stops adapting altogether and starts dying from lack of oxygen.

There was another Puja ceremony scheduled that was similar to the one we'd done at Cho Oyu, when we asked for blessing and safe passage on the mountain. Given that the year before, sixteen Sherpas had died during an avalanche in the icefall and nobody was able to summit, this ritual took on special meaning. We rubbed flour on one another's faces and offered rice as a gift to the gods, blessing our crampons and ice axes. I had also brought along my Empower Nepali Girls banner to receive a blessing as well. Then, with the prayers completed, we all started dancing, with Khumbu the dog barking hysterically and jumping around along with us.

Once the festivities ended, I realized how sick I was actually feeling. In addition to the vice-like headache that was squeezing my brain, I had a sore throat and felt completely lethargic. It was an effort to even stroll back to my tent and rest. Kate, sweetheart that she was, stopped by to check on me and brought a glass of warm salt water to gargle with, hoping it would soothe my throat. Even Khumbu seemed to notice I wasn't quite right, so he stood vigil outside my tent, where he lay down for his own nap.

When I awoke the next day, I felt much better, enough so that I could manage our scheduled acclimatizing hike up to Pumori Peak at 19,000 feet. In the Sherpa language, Pumori means "unmarried daughter," and it is often referred to as Everest's little daughter. Although it is not very technical or difficult compared to the "big father" next to it, close to fifty people have lost their lives in avalanches trying to get to the top.

Practice and Training

I was quite aware that climbing Everest was not like anything I'd ever attempted before. Sure, I'd been at high altitude on Cho Oyu, which was almost comparable, but the additional few thousand feet in the "death zone" made this climb infinitely more difficult. In addition, a fair bit of technical climbing would be required, not just to get through the icefall but also on the Hillary Step right before the summit. Then there were all the crowds that were vying to get to the summit—dozens of different teams from various countries would slow us down while we waited for struggling climbers to negotiate certain parts that we could only pass through one at a time. Sometimes people have to wait in line for hours to get through certain sections. That's when people freeze to death, or their window of opportunity closes.

We were scheduled to spend the next week practicing and training, testing our endurance and skills so the guides could assess our readiness. They took us out on ice walls to practice crampon and axe techniques. We practiced rappelling off cliffs, crossing ladders in our heavy boots with all our equipment, and self-arrest techniques if one of us slipped off a glacier or fell into a crevasse—all very real possibilities. The one thing we didn't prepare much for were avalanches, because frankly, in much of the terrain, there's not much you can do except pray.

Even though it felt like in some ways I was living in a vibrant city, with all the noise, parties going on, music blaring, and conversations I could hear through the walls of my tent, I was often reminded that we were all sitting in a very precarious, isolated, wild part of nature. The howling winds pummeling the tent were so strong during a few of the nights that there was no way to get any sleep. I kept thinking all night long about what I'd do if the wind just lifted me up and dropped me in a crevasse.

Even with the trouble sleeping and chronic headache, I still had to remain focused on our grueling training regimen. We would go into the Khumbu Icefall most days and practice safety techniques and crossing ladders as fast as possible. This is one of the most dangerous places in the world, where fissures in the ice open with no warning, toppling ice towers as tall as buildings that guard the entrances to routes up and over the obstacles. More people die here than anywhere else on the mountain, and it's almost always a random, unavoidable set of circumstances. So whenever I was in this magical, beautiful, dangerous place, it felt like I was holding my breath, waiting for something really bad to happen. While navigating ourselves through, around, and over the ice barriers, I was constantly thinking about how this mountain could swallow me up in an instant: one minute I'd be striding along; the next moment the ice would split open and I'd fall through.

The worst part of our exercises involved crossing the ladders suspended over open crevasses. Sometimes, two ladders are lashed together because the opening is too wide; at other times, the ladders are attached at a slight angle or tipped upward so we can crawl over a wall. Just imagine how terrifying it might be to walk across a ladder suspended over an endless gaping hole in the ground, one that is so deep that even if you had the courage to look straight down, you wouldn't see the bottom. Now picture doing this while wearing huge, unwieldy, heavy boots with the soles lashed to a dozen sharp spikes that clank awkwardly with every step. Add to this challenge that you are also wearing a heavy fifty pound backpack, throwing your center of gravity off balance. Oh yes—it could also be wickedly icy on the ladder in a blizzard, and the wind could be blowing at fifty miles an hour.

Camp One

It was finally time for us to start relocating ourselves up to Camp One, which made me nervous because that meant we'd have to get all the way through the icefall and then back again after some acclimatizing time. On our first attempt, our plan was just to make it as far as we could and then turn back, just so we'd become more familiar with the terrain and more comfortable balancing ourselves when we crossed the ladders. This was so much harder than I'd thought it would be when I had practiced at home. For one thing, sometimes I could feel the glacier shifting. Secondly, the ladders were often wobbly and felt unstable. And thirdly, the rungs on the ladders weren't always a uniform distance from one another, so it meant that each step with crampons had to be carefully planned—and this required looking down frequently; peering into the abyss gave me vertigo.

Everyone on our team was encouraging, Aussie Jon most of all. He was just always cheerful about everything, as if he didn't have a care in the world, and this felt contagious and reassuring. His tent was a little bigger than the rest of ours, so he called it "the mansion" and would frequently invite us over to play games or hang out.

Just before we were about to leave on the second attempt, I confessed to Aussie Jon that I was scared about our trip so far into the icefall. There was something disconcerting about the idea that at any minute the earth could open its mouth and eat me or a huge building of solid ice could fall on top of me. "You can do this," he reassured me. "We'll take care of one another. The odds of falling into a crevasse are pretty remote—and even if that happens, we'll just pull you out." Then he grinned and, in that typical Australian way, lightly punched me in the arm and said, "No worries, mate."

I went back to my tent and felt I was finally ready to read the letter that my friend Pari had given me at the airport with instructions to read it when I was having some doubts and fears. Truthfully, I was terrified going through the icefall. Yes, it was gorgeous. Some of the time, it was really fun climbing up ice towers and traversing the jigsaw puzzle pieces of ice that sometimes blocked our way. But there was also something formidable and menacing about the place. With every step, I wondered if I was walking on top of someone else's buried body.

In the letter, Pari reminded me that I chose to be vulnerable and take a risk in beginning this whole enterprise. She told me that I wasn't doing this alone, although sometimes it felt that way. That she was with me. That all my friends and family were with me. I burst into tears as I tucked the letter back into my duffel and started organizing my equipment for the next day's departure. It would be April 25, and so far I'd been in Nepal for a month.

We woke up really early the next morning to have breakfast because it was going to be a long, tiring day. My backpack was loaded with all the stuff I'd need for a few days before we returned, and I felt wobbly just trying to remain upright until I could find my stride.

In some ways, it was almost a relief that the visibility wasn't that great because of blowing snow, as it helped me to keep my focus only on looking at the small space right in front of my next careful step. We made excellent progress, keeping up a slow, steady pace. Although it was approaching midday, it was bitterly cold. My legs were tired, but I was still feeling strong.

I stopped for a moment to look around and remind myself of where I was and how I had gotten there. It was a wonderland of ice, as if a mad sculptor went wild, creating deep, yawning caves, towers and blocks of frozen walls, and fractures that seemed to sink to the bottom of the earth.

The truth was that I was terrified every moment we were stuck in this killing zone, and I was counting the minutes until we would reach safety. I couldn't help but think about all those who had perished in the icefall—crushed by falling ice towers, lost in hidden crevasses, wiped out by avalanches, carelessly falling off ledges. One part of me kept whispering, "easy steps," but there was also a much louder voice that was screaming, "Get me the hell out of here!"

I'd crossed so many ladders that I'd lost count—certainly over fifty of them, each one either leaning over a crevasse or propped up against a wall. I much preferred the vertical ones because if I fell, there was at least a chance I could survive as long I was solidly anchored. The deep, long canyons were the worst, with three or four ladders lashed together as a rickety bridge that bowed in the middle. I just kept reminding myself to not look down and take lazy, relaxed, deliberate steps. I heard the scrape of my crampons on the aluminum rungs and concentrated on carefully placing each foot; if I slipped, I would likely take out the climbers right behind me.

Just as I got to the top of a ladder, I'd yell out, "Clear" in a hoarse voice I hardly recognized. That was my signal that it was safe for those behind me to follow as I started up the next ladder to reach the ledge where we would rest.

The route through the icefall had been completely changed this year as a result of the worst climbing tragedy in history on the mountain. The previous year, more than a dozen Sherpas had been carrying equipment and supplies early in the morning—generally a reasonably safe time to do this work—when an avalanche swept off the west shoulder and buried them all. It's likened to playing Russian roulette because survival is based on random conditions that are completely out of one's control.

We were now following the new pathway that wound through and around the various obstacles standing in our way. And things were going very well indeed: our team was strong—no weak links and each member able to support the others. It was snowing. And even with our late start, we were making good progress toward Camp One and would certainly arrive in just a few more hours.

I could feel almost constant movement and shifting on the ladders, even when they were bolted firmly into the ice. Sometimes they slipped a little from the weight of one or more of us climbing upward or across. The ice itself was always moving, making groaning sounds that almost sounded human.

Every footstep was like walking in a field of landmines, never knowing when I might fall through. My back was killing me because my pack was so heavy on my shoulders: I was now carrying all my supplies, clothes, and equipment up to Camp Two which would soon become our new base. Since all the other teams had left before us, we were rushing to catch up.

Finally, we reached a towering ice wall just ahead. Camp One was located on top of the ridge. Now we just had to negotiate five vertical ladders that were connected to one another and attached to the wall rather than use our ice axes and crampons to climb the ice. The ladders made this stage so much easier.

We took one last rest perched on top of a serac, an ice tower with a flat top that we'd had to climb over. We were all too tired to talk, so we just sat there, numb, trying to drink some water and eat a snack. We would be arriving at Camp One in a few hours.

Damian went first on the ladders, then Jon, then I would follow next. When I heard Jon yell, "Clear," it meant he was off the rope and ladder, so it was my turn. I stopped for a moment to look around and grinned at my team-mates waiting at the bottom. For the first time in a while, I felt really strong, really good. We were at 20,000 feet, and I realized I no longer had any altitude symptoms. I don't know if it was my excitement, my newfound strength, or some premonition, but I scurried up those ladders just as fast as I could climb, just wanting to be on solid ground again instead of suspended in space.

I was almost at the top, my arms and legs feeling rubbery, my breathing labored, when all of a sudden I could feel the ladder start to vibrate, then shake and begin to pull loose from the wall. I held on as tightly as I could, but it felt like the whole world was ending.

What was that sound?

Inside a Blender

Sara
April 2015

I resettled myself into a more comfortable position and reached up for the next rung of the ladder. I grabbed hold and was preparing to lift up when I could feel that something was terribly wrong. I was certain the ladder was still attached to the wall, yet I could feel everything shifting and shaking to the left, then to the right. I could feel myself falling, and yet holding tighter didn't seem to be helping much at all; it was as if the whole mountain was falling. And it was.

All of a sudden, it felt like I was inside a blender with whirling snow everywhere and a strong wind that was threatening to blow me off the wall. My brain couldn't process what was happening, and I wondered why everything was suddenly exploding all around me. All I could think to do was grab onto the rope above the ladders and try to pull myself to safety. I could hear someone below screaming, "Avalanche!"

I was climbing just as fast as I could up that last ladder, pulling on the rope above me, hoping to get to the top before the wall collapsed completely. I looked over my shoulder and saw ice towers falling everywhere. The place where we had stopped for a break just a few minutes earlier was now gone. Completely vanished. If we had rested just another few minutes there, we'd all have been swallowed up by the blinding hurricane of snow.

Big chunks of ice were breaking off to my left and right. I lost all visibility and could now feel the brunt of the avalanche itself burying everything in its path. There was debris and blowing snow everywhere, making it difficult to orient myself. All I cared about was going up, up, up until finally, I pulled myself over the edge of the wall on my chest. I was hyperventilating, breathing so hard I thought I was going to pass out. I couldn't get enough oxygen into my lungs, and every time I did try to draw a breath, it felt like I was drowning. I clipped myself into as many of the anchors and carabiners as I could find, realizing that would do little good if the whole wall collapsed. The wind was blowing so hard I thought I'd take flight, so all I could think to do was hug the ground, which was bucking like a bronco.

I wrapped a rope around my hand and arm and tied it off to an anchor, thinking that if and when the wall fell down into the crevasse below, I might be able to save myself and climb back out. I was so cold that I could barely grip the rope. My nose and mouth were smothered, as if a cold towel was held over my face. My heart was pounding so hard I thought that I might be having a heart attack. I had to keep reminding myself to hang on and breathe. I remembered to put my hand in front of my mouth so after I was buried I'd have an extra few minutes of oxygen before the air ran out.

I knew the avalanche was just about on top of me, as I could feel the whipping wind becoming even stronger. I held onto the rope as tightly as I could and started kicking the spikes of my crampons into the ice to help further stabilize me. There was a moment of complete silence when everything seemed to pause for a moment—and I realized I was about to die. I had a sudden thought, wondering if my friends and family would erect a memorial for me in that graveyard I passed. Then I concencentrated on holding onto the rope with all my strength.

I kept saying to myself, over and over, *This is how people die here.* I realized that even with all my training, nothing could have really prepared me for this. I had time to think about the sadness my family would feel, what my husband would do; my last thought was wondering if they would ever find my body. Strangely, I felt at peace. I just held on as tightly as I could and waited for whatever would come next.

Through the screaming wind and sounds of crashing ice, I could hear one of the guides yelling up to me, asking if I was okay. I could hear others screaming their locations. But I couldn't move. Whatever calm I had felt had blown away with the raging wind and snow that had somehow passed over me. I was in an advanced state of panic. I was shaking so badly that I couldn't control myself. My legs wouldn't work. All I could do was clench and unclench my hands as they held onto the rope. I tried to take a deep breath, and I started sobbing. Even more terrifying to me was that I didn't know why I was sobbing. I was completely out of control, as if something else was inhabiting my body. It was like something had changed in me. I felt like a two-year-old child who had just fought with an eighteen-year-old and lost. I felt small. I didn't feel safe; I might never feel safe again.

Most of the ladders below us were broken or had fallen into crevasses. Others were so unstable that it wasn't safe to go back down. We were trapped, completely cut off from the world. The thought occurred to me that with the winds and blowing snow, not to mention our altitude, even a helicopter wasn't an option. There would be no way to rescue us; we were on our own, with limited food and supplies. Maybe we could last a few days at this altitude, time enough to make peace.

I noticed a head peek above the edge of the wall and recognized my tent-mate, Kate. Her face was grim but determined as she held up her hand to me and said, "I can't feel my fingers. I'm so cold. I think my fingers are gone." As I started to crawl over to her, I felt the mountain shift once again, and I grabbed on tighter to my rope. Was that an aftershock of what I now recognized had been an earthquake that had unleashed the avalanche?

I started to freak out even more after recognizing my friend, thinking that this mother of four might lose all her fingers. Somehow that struck me as even more terrible than our merely being buried alive. I started to hyperventilate again and couldn't catch my breath. I flipped over on my back and saw nothing but the swirling snow above me.

Somehow, during the next few hours, our team miraculously found one another. Apparently everyone had survived, yet I couldn't stop crying. I could hear over the radio that many people still in Base Camp had been crushed by boulders and ice from the avalanche. I learned that those above us were trapped and couldn't get down. We were trapped up here, and there was no way down. The ladders had vanished, and we were now stranded in the death zone.

14

All is Lost

Sara
April–May 2015

Once our team had regrouped on the ridge at the top of the wall, we stood holding one another. Reports were now coming in via radios and satellite phones about the extent of the damage throughout Nepal. It had been a 7.8 earthquake, one of the most devastating the region had ever seen. Over one hundred thousand children were left homeless, thousands buried under rubble in Kathmandu. The whole country was reeling from the death and destruction.

I assumed that by now, friends and family back home had heard the news and must believe I was gone, swallowed by the icefall. Initial reports portrayed the fatalities on Everest as catastrophic. We heard that dozens of bodies were strewn around base camp, buried under huge boulders, torn apart. There were reports that those of us caught in the icefall had also perished. The mountain had once again shut down all attempts to climb her, and it would be a second year with nobody making it to the summit.

Although all I wanted to do was sit down in the snow and rest, the guides kept urging us further upward to safety. There was no trail anymore; everything had been wiped out by the avalanche. There were more ladders to climb, but now they were wobbly, unstable, barely anchored to the ice. We worried about the people below us and above us: how could they have possibly survived? Our only option was to keep moving upward because there was nothing left below us.

Once we arrived at the high camp, the first thing I noticed was one of the guides from another team standing in front of a tent, crying. He had just heard the news about all the people who had died at Base Camp. A rolling avalanche had virtually wiped out almost everyone and everything in its path.

Climbing to Safety

I don't know how I managed to climb the ladders and proceed higher for the past three hours until we reached Camp One at 20,000 feet. As we trudged forward, I kept telling myself to take just one more step. The saving grace was that I was so numb, physically and emotionally, that my body was functioning on autopilot and I was somewhere else far, far away.

I collapsed, falling forward onto my face. The camp doctor, Julie, took one look at me and realized how much trouble I was in. My brain was scrambled and so traumatized that I'd lost track of where I was and what I was doing there. I was lost and disoriented, shivering as much from terror as the penetrating cold that was settling in. I had somehow pulled myself together enough to climb up to the camp, but once I saw the remnants of our crew, I completely lost control.

Dr. Julie forcibly picked me up off the ground, yelling through the gale-force winds, "Sara. Sara! You have to get inside or you are going to die!" She dragged me, pulling me inside a tent, and began to undress me, untying my boots and crampons—no easy task, considering that the laces and straps were frozen solid. I was shivering, shaking, still sobbing.

Julie kept talking to me in a reassuring voice—something about the expedition the previous year when a similar tragedy happened. "Most of those same climbers are here with us now. Once again, they'll have to go home."

"Go home?" I couldn't make sense of what she was talking about. "Aren't we here to make it to the summit? Why would we go home?"

Julie looked at me like I was crazy—which I suppose I was. "I'm hungry," I said. "I need some food."

Julie just shook her head. "Sorry. I don't have any food. But you need to rest." She started to rub my shoulders. The last thing I remember before passing out was the sound of Julie's voice telling me everything would be okay.

Hoping for Rescue

Hours, maybe just minutes later, I awoke from my stupor to the sound of voices outside, frantic voices sharing scraps of information about all the people who were dead, the villages destroyed. Once I managed to reassemble myself, physically and mentally, I changed into dry, warm clothes. I stepped outside and learned that my worst fears were confirmed: we were all now trapped on the mountain above the clouds, with limited supplies and food to sustain us. There was no longer any way back through the icefall, and some people were saying that they didn't think a helicopter rescue at this altitude and in these conditions was even possible. Even if we could somehow make it back to Base Camp, there was no longer any trail for the weeklong walk back to the airport in Lukla, from where we would be able to journey home.

I crawled back into the tent and passed out once again. I was awakened several hours later by another earthquake and the roar of an avalanche barreling down on Nuptse, the mountain right next to us. I could hear one of our guides yelling at us to close our tents and keep our helmets on at all times in case the tents broke loose. I could feel the tent whipping back and forth against the wind, straining to hold on to its moorings. Every few minutes, pieces of ice would slam against the sides. I just gripped my ice axe and hoped that if everything broke loose I could somehow anchor myself.

For two nights, I stayed trapped in the tent, hoping and praying that we weren't forgotten—that they'd send a rescue team, although I couldn't imagine how they would get to us. Most of the time I was so exhausted and cold that all I could do was just stay huddled in my sleeping bag with all my clothes on. I still couldn't stop crying. Aftershocks were now coming every few hours, making us even further terrified that we wouldn't last until maybe a helicopter could (hopefully) make it up to retrieve us. I kept thinking about my family: how much they would be worried about me and wondering if I was still okay. But most of all, I worried about all the girls down below and how they were managing—if they had lost their homes, if they had even survived.

Kate and I tried to comfort one another. She had been through something similar the previous year, even though her life had not been in immediate jeopardy.

I heard Orion and Aussie Jon outside my tent having some kind of discussion and peeked outside with Kate to see what was going on. Yup, still snowing and blowing.

"Hey," Jon called out, "'ya want to go higher?"

Kate and I just looked at one another. Was he saying he still wanted to try for the summit? We just shrugged. We knew how disappointed he must be. This was the second year in a row he got close and couldn't make it. "Whatever the team decides," Kate called out. But we knew he wasn't serious, just annoyed at all the bad karma.

All kinds of rumors were circulating about what had happened below, how many had died, and who may have survived.

To keep us calm, the guides were trying to pretend everything was normal, that they had everything under control. Eric was melting snow to give us some hot water, while Damian was trying to set up a rescue team to check the crevasses. Their professionalism had kicked in, and I suppose that did help to reduce the panic I was feeling.

I mentioned to Damian that I was feeling really sick and nauseous, that I hadn't eaten anything in the last day except a few almonds. Keep in mind that you burn about ten thousand calories a day during high altitude-climbs, so I was running on fumes. I could feel my body shrinking.

I slipped back into my tent to rest when I heard Eric scream in a hoarse voice, "Avalanche! *Avalanche coming!* Close your tents! Put your helmets on!"

Sure enough, I could hear the roar of an avalanche bearing down on us. I had only a few seconds to try and lace up my boots and put my jacket on. The ground was rumbling, then shaking madly. This was it. No escape this time.

It turned out that the avalanche was right next to us on Nuptse, and we were feeling the aftershocks of another earthquake.

A few seconds later, Eric yelled out again—or, more accurately, whispered like an old man because his voice was so hoarse—"It's okay. We're fine."

The time we spent waiting for a possible rescue was agonizingly slow. There was nothing to do but worry and feel sorry for ourselves. Whatever news we received from the satellite phones was dire and even more depressing. Whole villages were gone. Kathmandu had been devastated. And it was confirmed that landslides had completely destroyed the trail back. We were totally at the mercy of others who may or may not ever arrive. We learned that three Sherpas had tried to find a way back down through the icefall to create a new navigable trail but were buried in another avalanche. Things seemed more dire and hopeless than ever.

During one of the rare times I actually fell asleep, I heard a muffled sound outside—the mechanical sound of rotors, which could only mean a helicopter was landing somewhere nearby. Unless I was hallucinating.

Kate and I opened the flap of our tent and looked outside. Sure enough, a helicopter had managed to get to us. At this altitude, the air was so thin and the winds were so treacherous that the aircraft could only manage to ferry two people at a time. They wanted to begin by taking the lightest and smallest among us first, just to make sure they could take off again. It was one of the first times I remember feeling grateful for my small size.

As the helicopter took off, I looked back to see my friends and teammates waving. I felt so relieved that I would be saved, but I felt badly for those left behind. There was still a question about how many flights would be able to successfully ferry people back and forth, especially with the weather so tenuous and the continuous aftershocks that were still rocking the landscape. If anything, the wind and snow seemed to be getting worse. I might never see any of them again.

Back to Base Camp

It took just a few minutes for the flight to land, after which it immediately took off again to retrieve more climbers stranded above. Eventually, the fleet would end up making more than a hundred flights back and forth, dropping off supplies and carrying passengers two at a time. Fortunately, that was one part of the experience that seemed to go reasonably well. And I'm so incredibly grateful to the pilots who risked their lives to save us.

Just a few days earlier, Base Camp had been as happy as Disneyland, with everyone so excited about their upcoming summit attempts. It had been party city, with music blaring and people staying up most of the night, talking, drinking, telling stories about their prior adventures, and comparing notes about their world travels. Now it was a ghost town, and the ghosts were still very much present. I could see blood-spattered clothes on the ground; huge rocks had crushed tents with everyone inside. Brightly colored gear was scattered all across the mountain, and the survivors were wandering around, searching for their friends' bodies.

About the only good news was that I had Internet access again and could catch up on the news and communicate with all my friends and family back home, reassuring them I was safe. There were several messages from Jeffrey reporting that the girls were mostly safe—a few were missing—and all of them were asking about me. He was already in the process of organizing relief efforts, raising money, and purchasing supplies and medical equipment. He asked me to be his eyes and ears and scout what was most needed. He also wanted me to tell everyone that help was on its way.

The news of the disaster had gone global, and Jeffrey said he and his team were on their way, but he needed to know more about what was happening. He was hoping for a detailed report once I'd returned to Kathmandu. I had been feeling so sorry for myself that this new mission helped me to focus on something positive. Since we had to remain at Base Camp for most of another week before we could arrange a helicopter back to Lukla, we were stuck at the scene of the disaster. I now had a new job: to contact as many of the girls as I could and help them.

Most of the other climbers spent time commiserating about their failed summit attempt, some for the second year in a row. Everyone was emotional. Most people remained isolated in their tents, in no mood to socialize. Symptoms of post-traumatic stress were rampant. It was not uncommon to see someone walking around in a daze with tears streaming down his cheeks or muttering to himself.

One subject of conversation that seemed endlessly fascinating to everyone was the mystery surrounding one of the climbers who had died, some guy named Dan who had been working on a secret project for Google. People kept speculating about what he was really doing in camp, since he had been involved in a bunch of unusual things related to self-driving vehicles, balloon-powered Internet access, and something called Google Adventure, which aimed to map remote areas. Who knows? Maybe he was setting up a Google Maps walking route or a chairlift to the top of the mountain. It was a welcome distraction.

Most days, we just went for walks around the camp, looking for those who needed help or who'd lost all their belongings and needed clothes or food. I spent a lot of time with a few of the other Iranian climbers because I found that I wanted to speak in Farsi about what had happened. I needed to ground myself, to make myself more comfortable in familiar surroundings.

There was a lot of extra food that had been saved for summit attempts, and I tried to collect as much of it as I could for the girls. I made the rounds around camp, begging everyone for extra food that I could distribute to families that were probably starving. I made a point to avoid looking at the ground as much as possible because sometimes I'd catch a glimpse of a blood-stained jacket or even what I suspected might be a body part.

Please Don't Forget Us

After so many days waiting, we finally landed in Lukla Airport before transferring on to another helicopter that would take us back to Kathmandu. Unfortunately, that meant I couldn't check in with the children along the trail to Base Camp, so I hoped that Jeffrey would be able to do so in a few days when they arrived in the country. I knew that Jeffrey was collecting supplies and assembling a trauma team and would be departing shortly.

As soon as the helicopter landed, I rushed out the door and started making my way to the children's homes nearby, or what was left of them. One of the girls, Manila, recognized me right away and escorted me around the village so I could check on the children and distribute food where it was most needed.

I was dumbfounded to see kids playing in the middle of the rubble like nothing had happened. Most of the houses were damaged in some way: missing roofs, collapsed walls. Most people were busy trying to put the debris together to make a shelter for themselves for the night. All around the village, people were assuming there were more earthquakes coming, so they were trying to do their best to prepare by collecting water, food, and blankets.

As I was leaving each home I visited or each child I recognized, they would say the same thing: "Please don't forget us." I promised them, reassured them, that I would indeed be back. That I would never, ever forget them. I told them I would help them to rebuild their homes and schools—and their lives.

"But *when* will you return?" they asked again. I told them that honestly, I wasn't yet sure, but Jeffrey would be there in a few days, and he would bring help.

Once we landed back in Kathmandu, it was confirmed that the devastated Everest area was only one region that had been affected by the earthquake. The capital city, thousands of years old and filled with ancient monasteries and temples, was now wrecked beyond belief. The tectonic plates underneath had literally lifted the city several feet and shifted it ten feet further south, knocking down so many of the ancient structures made of brick and mud. So many of the scholarship girls who had been working so hard to create opportunities for themselves were now left with nothing.

I Can Still Hear the Children Screaming

Jeffrey
May 2015

It had been two weeks since the first major earthquake. Sara had finally made it back home, and I was heading to Nepal with a trauma team. There had been little sleep for me during this interval because of the twelve-hour time change, which meant that I was receiving messages from children in the middle of the night.

"My house is gone," one twelve-year-old girl wrote. "I can't find my parents. I don't know what to do. Please help me!" Others were saying that they had no food or water and asked where they should go to find help.

There was absolute chaos throughout the country. Under the best of circumstances, Nepal only has marginal political stability and barely competent leadership. A ten-year civil war had led to a half dozen factions that were almost always fighting with one another. Whoever was supposed to be in charge had disappeared, likely in hiding, but he kept issuing contradictory proclamations. Kathmandu was in shambles. The streets were blocked with rubble, so transportation was at a standstill; even during the best of times, the traffic is a nightmare. Electricity, water, and sanitation facilities were no longer functioning. The Chinese border was closed because of landslides and avalanches in the mountains. The Indian border to the south was blocked because of some political dispute between the countries. Nepal was completely isolated and cut off from the rest of the world.

I had been trying to coordinate relief efforts with our volunteers in Nepal as well as throughout the U.S. and elsewhere. Everyone and anyone who'd heard about the disaster was calling for updates, wondering if Sara had survived. I had received brief messages from Sara once she made it back to Base Camp, giving me reports on what had happened and what was most needed.

Still recovering from her own trauma, she was in no condition to remain in the country for much longer, but her reports regarding the most urgent needs were valuable. The monsoon rains would soon be starting, so people would need tents, since it was unsafe to remain inside any building because of the frequent aftershocks. Food and clean water were in short supply; medical services were restricted only to certain areas.

Meanwhile, PayPal decided to assist with the disaster and adopted us as one of their preferred charities. Whereas normally our annual budget was fairly modest—distributing scholarships and supporting a few hundred children—within just a few weeks, hundreds of thousands of dollars were pouring in, allowing me to purchase necessities and supplies.

Several of my colleagues at the medical center helped me acquire bandages, splints, blood pressure monitors, IV sets, surgical equipment, and various medications. Another friend who was an infectious disease specialist sent me boxes of antibiotics, painkillers, and other medications that would be needed for the rampant infections. My home had become a warehouse for storing pharmaceutical and surgical resources: boxes were stacked up to the ceiling. So far, I had received permission from an airline to bring a "few" extra bags, but I could only manage to whittle down the basics to nine huge duffels that I intended to smuggle into the country.

I had heard that Nepali officials were turning back volunteers and were not allowing medical or relief supplies into the country unless they were paid hefty duties (bribes). Millions of dollars' worth of foreign aid and supplies that had not yet been allowed to enter through customs were sitting on the tarmac at the airport. Meanwhile, many people had no food, uncontaminated water, shelter, or even blankets to cover themselves. There were no working sanitation or toilet facilities in many areas, increasing the risk of spreading cholera, encephalitis, and other diseases because of all the bodies buried beneath the collapsed buildings.

Sara and I had just missed one another as I arrived in Kathmandu with a medical team composed of a former Navy Seal medic who was now working as a surgical assistant, a hospital administrator, and another friend who would function as a our pharmacist. Once we arrived in Kathmandu, we planned to recruit several of our former scholarship girls who were now nurses and could join our team along with some other volunteers who could help as translators and triage decisions.

I had expected all kinds of trouble getting our supplies into the country once we landed at the airport. Our plan was to pretend we were trekkers and that our duffel bags were filled with the usual hiking and climbing equipment, but it turned out that the airport was virtually abandoned. There was one guy who just waved us through passport control; nobody else was around to even check our bags.

We immediately headed to Pasang's home, which served as the organization's headquarters. Hundreds of children were waiting there with their families, not just to welcome us but to huddle together for safety. Our volunteers had erected a big tent, set away from any of the nearby buildings that could pose a danger during one of the many aftershocks. We were serving food and water as well as playing games with the children to keep them occupied.

Sara had returned home to spread word of the disaster in Nepal, which was already being relegated to old news. We needed to raise as much money as we could during the next few weeks in order to help families resettle themselves in temporary housing. The torrential rains were about to begin, and hundreds of thousands of people were now homeless and without any resources. We needed to distribute clean water, food, sanitation supplies, tents, blankets, clothing, and medical supplies and services to those who had been injured. Given that the government was being so uncooperative, the shortages of food, medicine, and fuel were about to become a lot worse. There would be miles-long lines of buses and cars waiting for three or more days in order to obtain a few gallons of petrol on the black market.

We'd only been in Nepal a few hours, jetlagged out of our minds yet doing our best to interact with the children and keep our wits about us in case one of the leaning buildings around us collapsed. I was entertaining a few of the younger children, playing games with them. I was holding hands with four young children between the ages of three and seven, playing "Ring Around the Rosie." We circled round and round before falling in a giggling heap on the ground. We chanted over and over, pulling one another in a ragged circle. That this nursery rhyme is sometimes attributed to a description of the "rosy rash" of the Great Plague in Europe (as well as the cremation of bodies) escaped me at the time. But as we rested, looking around at the hundreds of others gathered together for the free medical clinic we had organized, I felt the earth start to tremble and then buckle underneath, throwing us to the ground. I heard children screaming and crying, and I was distracted by the realization that I was no longer standing but sitting in the grass. I looked up to see buildings swaying violently, cracks in the walls appearing like spidery webs, bricks falling, structures crumbling. Everyone was running away from the buildings in terror, fearful that they would be crushed like the thousands of others who had died in the quake two weeks earlier. I was holding onto the children, trying to soothe them.

It had been another major earthquake: 7.5 on the Richter scale. The epicenter was about fifty miles away near the Tibetan border, a locale that I would soon visit with our medical/trauma team to provide the only assistance they would see in the foreseeable future.

Like a Nuclear War

The Nepali government was asking all foreign aid workers to leave the country. Thus far, I hadn't seen many relief workers anywhere except for a few Red Cross representatives from Europe and Japan, who were now preparing to exit because they were not welcome. Pretending our team members were trekkers and our dozens of duffel bags were filled with climbing equipment instead of surgical supplies, antibiotics, and other medications, we kept a low profile when taking off in a small plane toward Lukla, the gateway to Everest, the place Sara had previously departed.

We landed safely in Lukla, but the place seemed mostly deserted. After exiting the plane, we put on our packs and began walking on what used to be the Everest Base Camp trail but was now reduced to washed-out, broken hillsides. Avalanches had virtually wiped out most of the usual route, requiring us to walk along precarious cliff faces where teahouses and homes once stood but now were covered in rubble. The mud used as mortar between the stone huts had virtually liquefied, crumbling the structures into piles of rock. In many cases, they formed the graves of family members who had been trapped inside.

A few of the children Sara had visited before leaving immediately recognized me and Pasang and ran to greet us with huge smiles. "You didn't forget us," they screamed. "You came here like Sara said you would."

A few of the girls took us by the hands and led us to what was left of their homes. The first one we visited had a collapsed wall inside; part of another wall was missing altogether. But they had set up a make-do kitchen on the ground and invited us to duck inside for tea. Typical of most Nepalis I've known, they refused to complain or even appear to feel self-pity. They were just delighted to entertain visitors, so they shared Sherpa tea (a mixture of tea, yak milk, butter, and salt) with us. Let's just say it is an acquired taste, one I have yet to develop.

After we caught up on news in the village, the girls escorted us to other homes so we might check to see how everyone was doing. There were no serious injuries for us to treat, and the only hospital in the region was located within reasonable walking distance, so our services would not be needed so close to the airport. Nevertheless, we distributed some of our supplies to those who needed them. Just as importantly, we reassured each of the scholarship girls and their families, as well as the principal and teachers in the local school, that we would help them rebuild their structures and their lives.

The sizeable donations we received through PayPal now allowed us to expand our operations way beyond our original charter. We were able to allocate earmarked funds solely for earthquake relief, and my soon-to-be successor agreed to take the lead and follow through on this commitment. On this trip, we had come prepared with all kinds of valuable supplies.

As we walked along our improvised trail, we distributed tents and sanitation supplies to people we found along the way. The schools we had supported all these years were now almost completely destroyed, but we used a few of their intact rooms to set up our medical and trauma services. All it took was hanging out a sign reading "Free Medical Clinic," and hundreds of people came streaming in from the hillsides. Most of them had never seen a doctor or nurse before and had never had their blood pressure or respiration checked, so they were fascinated by this opportunity to not only have their wounds dressed and their infections treated but also to have a real medical professional check them out. Matt, our medic, had operated previously during combat in the Middle East, so he was well prepared to deal with some of the chaos and "battlefield" conditions we encountered along the way.

Most of the children were shell-shocked and tearful—not at all surprising, considering that almost everything they'd ever known and every meager possession they'd had were now gone. Many of them had lost relatives. One of the scholarship girls told us that her grandfather had been so disturbed by the earth constantly moving and shaking that he'd thrown himself in the river, taking his own life. Each day, several dozen people were committing suicide, having given up all hope. Hundreds of others just keeled over from heart attacks, their brains and hearts unable to handle the constant stress and uncertainty.

We were supporting over one hundred scholarship girls in the Everest region, and they were easy to recognize because they were wearing our trademark Empower Nepali Girls down jackets in bright, primary colors. The girls I met along the trail kept asking about Sara—whether she was okay, whether she would return soon to see them. Sara is their heroine, the woman they someday wish to become—poised, self-assured, accomplished, strong, and not dependent on anyone. All their lives, their caste, their tribe, their gender and station in life, had set rigid limits on what they were permitted to do. In many parts of Nepal, women can't inherit land. Their families can't afford to send them to school, since boys are first given that opportunity. They are denied entry into the best schools, largely because their own education and resources are limited. But Sara gives them hope that they can change their circumstance and become engineers, teachers, mountaineers—anything they want.

Trauma, Trauma Everywhere

Before we departed for the Everest region, we made a plan with our team as to how we would function. Matt was in charge of organizing all our medical supplies. Pasang was taking care of all our logistics. I had prepared simple treatment manuals for responding to the most acute psychological trauma symptoms and the more severe cases that would start appearing in a few months. I wanted to distribute these guides to local teachers and community leaders, providing them with basic strategies for recognizing symptoms of post-traumatic stress and trauma as well as simple techniques for responding to those who were suffering.

During my days of full-time practice as a psychologist, I used to think that seeing ten patients a day was challenging. Yet there were so many people in need of help that after setting up our clinic in two schoolrooms that were still standing, we treated 158 medical and forty-one counseling cases on our first day of operation. This meant that people were rotating in and out of my "office" an average of every fifteen minutes.

This was the first of five clinics that we planned to set up for the hardest-hit areas. People from all around the area lined up patiently outside. While Matt, our medic, Monet, our triage specialist, and two of the Nepali scholarship girls who were now nurses worked furiously to treat broken bones, abrasions, infections, wounds, and all kinds of trauma-related symptoms, I worked with various families, children, adults, and couples. At one point, there were so many people lined up at the door toward the end of the day that I just invited them all in for a group session. I used the time to encourage them to tell their stories and then taught them a simple mindfulness technique to calm down during one of the aftershocks or disturbing memories. We actually had an opportunity to practice together when a particularly strong aftershock rattled the building. We all looked at one another and started laughing: it was as if the spirits were messing with us.

Pasang's sixteen-year-old daughter, Chhusang, acted as my interpreter and assistant. I talked to people about their nightmares, insomnia, hypervigilance, and struggles losing their homes. The few in the region who were willing to talk about their fears felt isolated and alone, as if they were the ones who were weak; one woman told me her husband and children accused her of being "cowardly" because she startled so easily and refused to enter their house, preferring to sleep outside.

I visited with two seventy-year-old friends who were together presenting various chronic medical complaints for which our medic and nurses had no treatments. They were both extremely hard of hearing, so I kept yelling (through Chhusang) that their symptoms became worse because of the stress they were under. I saw a family concerned about their five-year-old son, who had been trapped in a building during the first earthquake and was now mute.

I spoke with a woman who had really wanted to see our doc, but because he was busy, she had come to see me instead. She reached out her hands to hold my own and just looked into my eyes for the longest time. I wasn't exactly sure what we were doing, but I just followed her lead. Then, abruptly, she thanked me, smiled, and walked out the door, holding it open for an even older fellow who was shuffling in. He told me he was ninety-six years old and in remarkably good health for his age, but he thought his time had come and he was going to die soon. He just wanted me to know a bit about his life before it ended. He must have enjoyed our conversation, because later I saw him standing in line again for another session.

I spoke with two young mothers and their children who wanted to talk about their fears because they said nobody else would listen. They reported that most of their neighbors and family were acting as if things were normal, making it difficult to tell their stories.

I barely had time for a break to empty my bladder before I noticed the line outside my room getting longer, and the prospective patients were becoming anxious and restless. The tremors continued, making all of us nervous. In my head, I constantly rehearsed the safest route outside every time I felt the ground shake.

There were cases that were so far outside of my usual standards of care that I could only shake my head in wonderment. One man complained of vertigo, which made perfect sense to me because I had also been dizzy since the earthquakes, feeling as if the ground was constantly moving (which it was!). I reassured him the symptoms would go away, but he insisted on some medication to make him feel better. So I "prescribed" some little orange pills, one in the morning before breakfast and one in the evening before dinner. They were aspirin, but sometimes all you need is hope.

I welcomed a mother who had broken her arm saving her child from a collapsed building during the earthquake and was refusing to go to the hospital to get it X-rayed and fixed. Matt had sent her to me to persuade her to go; otherwise, she might lose the function of her arm. I tried to be gentle, but during the translation, Chhusang scolded her and told her she owed it to her child to take care of herself. I looked at Chhusang with awe and admiration: in the time we'd spent together, this high school girl was turning into quite the counselor herself.

I tried all kinds of things during the sessions: normalizing their fears, explaining about trauma and its symptoms, inviting them to share their stories, teaching deep breathing and relaxation strategies, introducing a little self-talk, encouraging them to talk to others, and literally holding them, but I found what often worked best, especially with the children, was sharing with them that I felt much the same way they did: out of control, scared, overreacting to any sound or movement. We mostly laughed about that together.

All of my professional career, I've been working with symptoms of trauma, including the lingering effects of child abuse, sexual abuse, neglect, violence, or natural disasters. I've written many books on the subject that summarize the research and optimal treatment strategies. I've taught classes and workshops on creative interventions for the symptoms: using mindfulness-based strategies, cognitive self-talk, support groups, or relational connections.

I had expected I'd have to adapt my treatment approaches to fit the rather unique situation that we now faced. Although I'd been to Nepal more than twenty times in the past fifteen years, I was still quite ignorant and misinformed about certain cultural traditions. My knowledge of the language was at about the same level as a preschooler's. I'd done lots of "brief therapy" before, but not when I was limited to fifteen-minute sessions because there were so many people clamoring for attention.

I was able to make adjustments and adaptations for these limitations, at least to a certain extent. But what caught me most off guard was that I was now experiencing many of the same symptoms reported by my patients. I was constantly on edge. I couldn't sleep, and when I did manage to fall unconscious, one of the frequent aftershocks would awaken me, with my heart pounding in panic. Most disturbing of all was that I would suddenly, and without warning, just start sobbing. This frightened me most of all because it was like someone, or something, inside me would just burst out in tears. Much of the time I didn't know what I was crying about, except for perhaps the cumulative horrors that I'd witnessed and experienced.

After all these years working in Nepal, there was always a part of me that separated myself from the people I helped. There was such a differentness between this world and my own, a gap I could never quite bridge.

After returning from a trip, I'd feel transformed, as if my life back home was shallow, materialistic, driven by ambition and achievement. I'd feel guilty going out for a nice meal or buying new shoes, thinking that the money I was spending on myself could save a child or two. The effects wouldn't last, but I liked myself so much better when I cared less for possessions and accomplishments and instead focused on my most cherished relationships. This was something I learned from my visits, but alas, the insights were fleeting and impermanent.

This trip was different. I'd only been in Nepal for a few days, but it felt like we were all in this predicament together. We were comforting one another. They were as much my teachers as my patients. I was experiencing my own debilitating symptoms of fear and trauma: startling at the slightest loud noise; always staying near a door; if possible, remaining as far as possible from any building that might collapse. I was having nightmares and recurrent flashbacks. I found myself talking as much to myself as to the families when I cautioned patience and pleaded with them to take care of one another. I understood for the first time, at the deepest possible level, what I'd been teaching academically most of my professional career.

Back Home

Sara
May 2015

When I arrived at the airport in Los Angeles, my family was there to greet me, showering me with flowers and signs welcoming me back. After hugging me, they started checking my fingers to make sure they were all still there. I didn't know what to say to anyone. I looked at my mom, and she seemed to have aged with worry. Once again, I felt terribly guilty, not only for the concern I'd inflicted on everyone but also because I was home and not with the girls who needed me so badly.

Before we were even settled in the car, the first question my family asked me was whether I planned to return to Nepal anytime soon. I shrugged and just stared out the window, but they could read the signs, and it made them mad. "That's ridiculous! You can't go back there ever again! That mountain almost killed you!"

I didn't know what to say. I just felt numb and empty, like I had left a part of myself on Everest, and I didn't know if I'd ever regain what I'd lost. I had planned to leave letters, notes, and little stuffed animals representing our scholarship girls near the summit, but all of those things were lost in the avalanche, blown across the Himalayas. Sitting at home, I just stared at my duffel bags stuffed with climbing equipment, the things I was able to retrieve. I couldn't bring myself to open the bags because every single item reminded me of what had happened and everything I wanted to forget. I just sat there and cried, something I'd been doing a lot.

My aunt called me from Iran to make sure I was safe and healthy. She asked me to promise her I would never return to Nepal. She told me it was time to have babies like a good Persian wife. My husband felt much the same way. A woman like me didn't belong in those mountains. "Sara," she scolded me, "soon you will be forty. It is time for you to settle down."

She was referring to her sister (my mother), who had already had four kids by the time she was twenty-seven. I was thirty-four, with no children in sight, unless we counted my three hundred surrogate daughters in Nepal.

"I'm not ready yet," I tried to explain. "I have some things I need to do first." I wasn't exactly sure what those things might be, and I was pretty certain I wouldn't be going back up on that mountain any time soon, but I also wanted—needed—to return to Nepal as soon as possible. I knew that Jeffrey had just arrived there, and he was going to actually help people who were so desperate. All I had done was try and fail to climb a mountain. What kind of inspirational lesson was that for the girls?

Everyone was worried about me. It was obvious I was not the same person anymore. Something had changed in me, and I wasn't clear yet what that was all about. I still felt crippled and traumatized, awaking in the middle of the night in terror.

When the feelings started flooding back, I felt such incredible shame and guilt that I had failed the climb, and the girls, so miserably. I was supposed to empower them with my efforts, and all I did was become a burden to the many brave people who rescued me. Meanwhile, I was back in my comfortable world with all the luxuries of electricity, hot water, fresh food, and clean water, and I thought constantly of all the children who were living outside with nothing except a blanket. The monsoon floods would be starting any day, and I couldn't imagine how people would cope. In a way, I envied Jeffrey, who was there helping people while I enjoyed luxuries and my ordinary routines.

It just felt unreal to be back in Southern California, an environment and culture that is about as different from Nepal and Everest as one could possibly imagine. My sense of space was distorted. I'd been used to sharing a freezing tent for the past month. Any other dwellings I'd passed on the way to Base Camp were tiny one-room stone-and-mud huts that slept families of four. I kept thinking about one of the last girl's homes I had visited. There didn't seem to be enough room for even one person to sleep there, but the girl, her parents, and her brother all managed to somehow share the space. Now, even that was gone.

I returned to our spacious apartment on the top floor of a gorgeous building with views of the Orange County skyline. There was such privilege and wealth all around me. Everyone driving around in their BMWs, Mercedes, and Porsches, seemingly on top of the world.

It felt unreal to be able to just open a faucet and have clean water come out or turn down the thermostat and feel the cool air. And the food? I'd lost so much weight that now I could indulge in all of my favorite Persian treats and stuff myself until I burst. And all the while, as I readjusted back home, I kept thinking about the children who were now living outside in the monsoon rains, scrounging for food, trying to put their lives back together.

When I talked with my friend Pari, she tried to reassure me that my guilt was unfounded and based on distorted and wholly unrealistic beliefs. She had been one of Jeffrey's students and was an excellent psychotherapist, skilled at challenging me without pushing me too hard.

"But you *did* empower the girls," Pari pointed out. "You raised all that money for them, far more than you—or anyone—ever imagined possible. And the only thing that could have stopped you from reaching the summit was the biggest earthquake ever recorded in that part of the world. I'd guess those girls are damn proud of you!"

I knew I was fortunate to have survived when so many others had perished, but I just couldn't allow myself to be happy when so many others were suffering. And truthfully, I was embarrassed to see all my friends and trainers at the gym and having to admit that I couldn't make it to the top. Everyone said they were so proud of what I had already accomplished, but nothing seemed to have much impact—until my friends reassured me that they were now totally on board with my mission to raise even more money for earthquake relief efforts. I knew that Jeffrey and the rest of our team were raising money to assist the earthquake relief and recovery efforts, and I wanted to do so much more.

A Woman Transformed

I was slowly recovering from the shock and could see the importance of fundraising now, when the memory of the earthquake was so fresh. I started to come to terms with my "failure;" after all, this feeling was so familiar to me after all my other calamities on previous mountains. I knew that the reason so few people do this sort of thing is because the challenge is so daunting, and the chance of success is directly related to perseverance and resilience.

I also realized I had a pretty interesting story to tell, one that could appeal to audiences. There are dozens of famous climbers who go around giving inspirational speeches and talking about their triumphs for a fortune in speaking fees. But my story was rather unique in that it transcended mere physical courage and achievement; this was a story that so many girls and women could relate to. If, or when, I ever reached the top of Everest (and the other Seven Summits) was beside the point; this was a tale about what almost anyone could do to make a difference in the world—if you just take the first small steps and then keep going no matter what challenges you face along the way. This wasn't the end of my story, merely an intermission before whatever came next.

Slowly, I started to feel a glimmer of hope. I could feel my energy and motivation starting to return, little by little. On the other hand, I didn't like myself very much. I'd lost my self-confidence. I complained constantly. I felt sad and moody, beyond a place that Pari could touch in our conversations. But when I thought about the women in Iran, Nepal, or elsewhere in the world who are treated so poorly and are not even allowed a basic education, it just made me furious and more determined to show them that we can be different in spite of the attempts to oppress us.

I'd been watching the news several times during the day to find out what was happening in Nepal. I knew that Jeffrey was out there somewhere, totally isolated, maybe even stranded, and I wondered how they were all doing. According to all the reports I heard and read, things were becoming increasingly worse, not better. People were living in tent cities without any sanitation facilities. There was no safe drinking water, and food was scarce. With the water supply compromised, terrible contagious diseases were spreading. And now the blockade at the Indian border was tightening because the governments were feuding about a new constitution that would be ratified in Nepal, one that renewed a dispute over territory that both countries claimed. That meant that fuel, emergency supplies, food, water, and medical equipment could only be delivered by plane, assuming they could get through customs.

Interrogations

Several weeks later, I went to visit my mother in Arizona. She had created an incredible birthday cake for me that was shaped exactly like Mount Everest. She had meticulously built the cake to scale, and pictures of the various stages of the climb had been printed on sugar paper and attached to the cake. Little photos of me standing outside my tent were pressed into the whipped cream, which looked just like snow. An Empower Nepali Girls flag was perched on top, just like the one I had always planned to plant when I reached the summit.

I had tears in my eyes—grateful tears, but sad ones as well. I was so appreciative of what my mother had done, yet it brought back all my feelings of disappointment once again.

"I want you to look at the cake," my mother said to me gently. "I want you to see that you're bigger than Everest and that you don't have to climb it again. You already put the flag on top of the mountain." Then, she, too, broke out crying, and we hugged one another.

A little later, while we were sitting at the table eating the cake, my sister said to me, fairly abruptly, "So, are you planning to go back?" My family was driving me crazy with this same question over and over.

I hesitated for a moment, knowing there was only one answer she wanted to hear. "I don't know," I finally said, just above a whisper. "I haven't decided yet."

I could see the flash of anger in her eyes. "I just don't understand how you can be so selfish!" she yelled at me. "You put all of us through such torture. We thought you were dead, for crying out loud!" Then both my parents and my sister started crying.

I didn't answer and kept my mouth closed. I didn't know what to say to them or even what I could say, other than that I was sorry I had put them through such anguish. They just didn't understand why I was so stubbornly focused on pushing my limits or testing myself. And like so many others within my community, they didn't understand why I was doing all of this for a bunch of girls in some obscure country halfway around the world that they'd barely heard of. "Why aren't you helping Iranian girls?" I would frequently be asked. "Don't you think your first priority should be to help your own people?" But I wondered: Who *are* my people? I'm very proud of my Persian culture and heritage. I love the Farsi language. Yet as concerned as I was about what had been happening in my native country, I believed strongly that offering support to marginalized girls was a global issue, unrestricted by any national borders or loyalty to one nation.

It wasn't until I was pushed by my family to declare I wouldn't return to Nepal or climb any more mountains that an idea came together for me. I'm not sure if it happened right there at the dinner table with my family or if it slowly took more concrete form over the following days. I realized that there were some valuable, if unintended, lessons in my story. Maybe what I really needed to teach the girls was that striving for a goal is not about attaining it the first time you try. After all, many of the girls had had so little educational support that there was no possible way they could pass entrance exams to university the first time they tried. It was resilience and persistence that mattered most. It was about not giving up no matter how difficult things get. I wasn't actually thinking about trying Everest again anytime soon, but I was considering how closely I was being watched by the girls to see how I handled my disappointment.

Redoubling My Efforts

Once I realized that my "climb" wasn't over and I could actually continue the journey working on behalf of the girls in Nepal as well as the earthquake relief, I started to plan ways I could help spread awareness of the current dangerous situation.

Since I was one of the "survivors" of the Everest disaster, media and news outlets were regularly contacting me for interviews. Everyone wanted to hear my story: I was the woman caught in an avalanche on Everest who was trying to bring greater awareness to the problems of neglected children. This led to increasing numbers of speaking engagements and media appearances. I was a novice at public speaking, but I did my best to just simply tell my story of what happened, talk about the challenges of the girls, and then ask people to help us by donating money for the cause and relief efforts. These events were packed, and the audiences were incredibly responsive and supportive. But it was hard. Maybe not as hard as having to slip out of a tent at 19,000 feet with fifty-mile-per-hour gale-force winds threatening to blow me off the mountain just to use the toilet facilities on the side of a glacier, but it presented some different challenges.

The first appearances had gone so well that I was singularly unprepared for one at a hiking/climbing store that was a terrible disappointment. Although more than sixty people had said that they would be attending, only a handful actually showed up, and I think those were people who just happened to be shopping in the store at the time. I noticed one such shopper standing in the back of the room with an armful of fleece jackets. Even worse, none of them decided to donate anything, even after hearing my most impassioned pleas and seeing tragic images of the children. I felt it was a colossal waste of time.

There was a familiar theme here: I was attempting a very difficult new challenge, just as I had when I was studying engineering, teaching computer science, or mountaineering. Initially, I enjoyed tremendous success and became cocky and overconfident, self-assured to the point that I expected everything to go as planned. Inevitably, there was some setback, disappointment, failure—perhaps an earthquake of sorts—and I became inconsolably discouraged. But I was determined to show courage and resilience, even in the face of impossible odds, because that's exactly what the girls face every day of their lives when they attempt to break the mold from which they were shaped.

Just like training for the mountains, the more I rehearsed and practiced my new skills as a fundraiser and public speaker, the more I was able to improve. If I was yet unable to attain the highest climb in the world, I felt such incredible pride and satisfaction in doing so on a very different stage. Quite literally.

I'd long been a fan of TED Talks, those inspirational and informative eighteen-minute online lectures that covered an incredible range of fascinating topics. Some of them had been viewed by tens of millions of people. So it was incredible to me that I was invited to come to Paris to deliver my own TED Talk about my experiences empowering girls and women. This was an Everest I never expected to climb!

I remember visiting an elementary school to give a talk. One third-grade girl came up to me afterwards and proudly announced that she had recently opened up her own personal savings account.

"That's great," I encouraged her, looking around for the door to make my exit. By now, the children had all dispersed back to their classrooms, but this one little ten-year-old girl was still looking up at me, waiting for something.

"Um, so I was saying," she continued, "I have, like, two hundred dollars in my account."

"I see," I answered, not seeing at all where this was going.

"So, I was thinking that because it's my own account and it's new and all—I told you I just opened it?"

"Uh-huh."

"Well, then I should probably leave at least a little money in the account. But I was wondering—I mean, would it be okay if I donated a hundred and fifty dollars to the girls?"

I was absolutely floored. My mouth fell open, and I just didn't know what to say.

"So, would that be okay?" she asked me again.

I just nodded my head.

"And when I grow up," she said, looking me right in the eyes, "I'm going to be just like you. I'm going to help poor people like you do."

Meanwhile, Back at the Epicenter of Another Quake

Jeffrey
May–June 2015

I'd been in touch with Sara back home, and I could tell she was suffering terribly, not just because of what she'd gone through on the mountain but also because she felt helpless, being so far away from what was now going on in Nepal. The place was an absolute wreck and becoming even more chaotic after the second big earthquake in the Everest region. People were wandering around in a daze, as if searching for their homes that had disappeared.

I should have known what I'd be getting into, given some of my prior experiences working in a country in which so few people outside of the capital have access to healthcare. I'd visited regions where people stood on the side of the trail begging trekkers for aspirin. I'd been to villages where almost every single person had a huge goiter growing out of their neck because they only drank glacial water and had no iodine in their diets. I recall years ago being in places so isolated that it took four days just to walk to the nearest bus and then another two days to reach the nearest medical facility. If you developed appendicitis, you died. A compound fracture from a fall? No chance to survive. Complicated pregnancy? Except for the local midwife, no other help available.

I thought about all of this as we carefully crept along a steep slope into a village where we could see everyone waiting for our arrival—word had spread that there were "doctors" coming to save them. Much of the trail was becoming increasingly difficult to manage after the mudslides and avalanches had made their mark. In this part of the world, these narrow trekking routes were the interstate highways, the only way that supplies could be delivered by mule or yak. With the trails washed out, they were all completely cut off, which explained why we were the only aid workers around. And honestly, we weren't in the best shape, trying to just survive the journey along these treacherous mountainsides, constantly looking over our shoulders for an escape route to take after the next quake, which could occur at any moment.

Some Rather Unusual Cases

We set up our medical clinic in an open field so there would be plenty of room for people to wait while we did our best to attend to as many patients as we could. In other locales, we had been able to operate in a tent or a schoolroom. In some cases, if the patient wasn't ambulatory, we'd make house calls. In each of them, Chhusang and I would set up shop in a separate area. One of our medical assistants was operating as our triage specialist, asking the long line of patients about their presenting symptoms, which usually included an infection and acute trauma along with hundreds of different medical issues that may or may not have resulted from the earthquake and its aftermath. There were terrible grief issues, with so many people having lost family members. We could hear almost everyone coughing because of respiratory infections. And almost everyone was absolutely exhausted and desperate from sleep deprivation and post-traumatic stress symptoms that included nightmares, unrelenting anxiety, startled responses, pounding hearts, depression, hopelessness, and despair.

My first patient of the day was quite unusual. The woman had been referred to me after Matt, our doc, signaled to me that he couldn't help her.

"Namaste," she said with her hands steepled into the traditional Nepali greeting.

I returned the greeting with a smile and asked how I could help her, after which she displayed her hand. Since I'm the psychologist on board, I wondered what I was supposed to do with it, so I looked back over at Matt, who just smiled and then went back to work on some surgery.

I learned through Chhusang's translations that she said her hand didn't work.

Okay, so what was I supposed to do for a broken hand?

"No," Chhusang explained, "her hand wasn't exactly broken. It just doesn't work."

"What do you mean, her hand doesn't work?" I asked. I sent Chhusang over to Matt to find out what was going on, and she returned to tell me that the woman's hand was paralyzed but he could find nothing medically wrong.

The bones and ligaments were all perfectly functioning, but the appendage was completely numb.

I began to question the woman and learned that at the exact moment of the earthquake, she had grabbed on to her mother's sleeve and held on as tightly as possible to steady them both as the building swayed back and forth, crumbling around them. Ever since then, her hand had had no sensation whatsoever.

Now what was I supposed to do? There was a lineup of impatient people waiting to get in to see me, and it was growing longer every minute. I was used to doing a half dozen fifty-minute therapy sessions during a typical day, and during these clinics, I was treating someone every few minutes. Time was racing along, and somehow I was supposed to fix her problem. I had no idea where to begin. This was like one of those cases of hysterical trauma among Victorian women that Freud described a century ago, a psychosomatic response to stress.

There was nothing in my fairly extensive repertoire of interventions that seemed to apply to this situation, so I remembered something I had once witnessed when working with indigenous healers in Africa, where magic and mystery were so much a part of the rituals. Any self-respecting healer or witch doctor would *never* resort to mere conversation for a cure, and this situation surely required something out of the box. So an idea came to me, a plan that struck me as a little crazy but also entirely appropriate.

"I'm so glad you came to see me," I first reassured the woman with a smile, the whole time rubbing her numb hand with my own. "I *do* know how we can fix this problem."

She looked up at me hopefully, completely trusting my judgment. It's sad to say that Westerners in this part of the world command the kind of respect and awe that would make my "placebo" cure even more powerful, since it relied on faith and strong belief. It was discovered long ago that doctors can prescribe sugar pills for ailments, and those pills can be antidotes just as powerful as those that are chemically active—*if* they are accompanied by appropriately persuasive reassurance. Faith and support are a strong part of *any* cure, which is why more than half the patients who consult with a physician don't actually have anything medically wrong—they just want a professional to tell them they'll be okay.

With this in mind, I explained to the woman that she must follow my instructions carefully. She readily agreed.

"Are you certain?" I asked her once again just to increase the power of what I was about to tell her to do.

Again, she nodded.

"Okay then, this is what you must do. Each morning when you awake, I want your mother to massage your hand with warm oil for a minimum of fifteen minutes. Is that clear?"

Enthusiastic nod.

"Good. And I want her to do the same thing each night before you go to sleep."

She looked over to Chhusang, who was staring at me with a look I couldn't interpret. I actually thought this would make some kind of sense in this culture because I remembered that during childbirth, the women relatives of the expectant mother take turns rubbing warm scented oil all over her body while they chant and sing.

"In addition," I continued, "I'm going to give you some very strong medicine that you are to take twice each day for the next three days, once in the morning before your mother massages your hand, and then before the evening hand rub. Is that clear?"

The woman smiled for the first time, "*Dhanyabahd, dheri, dheri dhanyabahd*," thanking me most effusively. I then proceeded to carefully count out the pills and place them in an envelope. They were actually just ibuprofen.

Like so many of the hundreds of people I treated during the next few weeks, I would never learn what happened to them, whether they lived or died, recovered or not. I wondered if hearing their stories was nearly enough. Yet it seemed so important to many people to have a chance to talk about their suffering and losses. Even when Chhusang wasn't around and I was required to conduct an interview in their native Sherpa language, it didn't seem to matter much whether we understood one another's words—we communicated through gestures and expressions.

I remember one older gentleman, well into his eighties, who had patiently waited in line for more than an hour in the hot sun to see me. Just as he entered the room and took a chair, Chhusang excused herself to take care of an errand, leaving us alone together. At first we just stared at one another, unsure how to begin, since we didn't speak one another's language. Finally, he reached out, took my hands, and leaned in close to me. I wasn't sure if he could even see me, since I noticed that his eyes were cloudy and leaking fluid.

Then he began to speak to me in a soft, whispery voice, and I listened intently, nodding my head occasionally in acknowledgment.

Finally, he smiled at me with a toothless grin, rubbed my hands affectionately, and thanked me. As I sat there wondering what had just transpired, I noticed the most remarkable thing: the man went to stand at the very end of the line to wait for another session!

This was actually a breakthrough for me, not only with respect to my work in Nepal but also how I would reconceptualize what I do as a speaker, psychologist, teacher, and even grandparent. I realized, more than ever, that my principal role was to hold and honor people's stories of suffering—and triumph—as well as to share the kinds of inspirational or motivational stories that might help them access greater resilience and inner strength.

A Cascade of Suffering

I had already seen four families in a row without a break, and my energy was faltering. Many cases were so similar: One or more of the children had a headache or stomachache or sleep problem, and the parents were worried. An adult was hypervigilant and overreactive to any noise or movement, unable to sleep or eat. Some preexisting medical conditions, like hypertension or heart problems, were now far more serious. There were so many people wanting attention and care that eventually I started seeing them in small groups, a half dozen or more at a time. I taught them a rudimentary form of deep breathing and a simplified form of self-talk, but mostly, I explained and normalized their reactions as typical of trauma symptoms and chronic, unrelenting fear. Once again, I shared with them that I was feeling much the same. They seemed to take comfort in the idea that we were all in this together.

Since many of the scholarship girls lived in this region, on occasion a familiar face would show up to say hello or report on how she and her family were doing. Almost all of them asked where Sara was, and I explained what happened on Everest and that she was at home recovering but would be returning to see them soon.

I was running out of energy—and hope—when a distraught mother approached me with her reluctant ten-year-old son in tow. She explained that her son refused to eat, and she was concerned about his health. He actually looked reasonably healthy, hardly anorexic. She was one of the few people I met who had actually consulted with doctors. They had ruled out any physical problem and diagnosed an eating disorder. This was something I'd not yet encountered in a country where the vast majority of the population doesn't have enough food to eat.

After a bit of questioning, I discovered that he was reasonably normal and happy in other ways, and the family was intact and healthy. Yes, their home had been damaged and they were living outside, but they planned to move back inside if there were no further quakes in the next few days. Besides, this refusal to eat had begun long before the earthquakes. Again, I felt the pressure to do something, fix this problem, especially since, by now, I was working inside a schoolroom that had been barricaded to keep the crowd of waiting patients from fighting to get inside.

I told the boy I had a test for him and wondered if he would pass. He looked intrigued, so I told him that I bet I could find something that he might like to eat. He barely looked at me, but I could see the beginning of a smile. I pulled out a Snickers bar and handed it to him. Out of pure obstinacy, he shrugged and passed it to his mother, pretending he wasn't interested. He looked back at me defiantly, the glimpse of a smile now gone.

"What *do* you like to eat?" I asked him.

He didn't bother to answer. Just shook his head.

"What about smoothies?" I remembered his mother had said that they'd visited Kathmandu to see doctors for his condition.

For the first time, he nodded his head in the affirmative—or rather waggled it back and forth in that characteristic Nepali way that is both an indistinct yes and no and also a maybe.

"What about KFC?" I always found it interesting that the single busiest, most popular restaurant in Kathmandu served fried chicken from the colonel.

Another nod.

"Kabobs?"

Again, a nod.

"So, what *don't* you like to eat?" This was not like any eating disorder I'd ever heard of.

He whispered something I couldn't hear. "Say that again," I prompted him. "*Dahl baht.*"

"I see." And now I *did* see. Most Nepali people eat rice and lentils for both meals of the day, every day, even when they are provided other choices. It is perhaps the single most nutritious meal that the human body could metabolize and provides a cheap and efficient source of protein and energy. It turned out he really didn't have an eating disorder at all; he just didn't like *dahl baht*, but he *loved* fast food.

I instructed the mother to vary his diet, recognizing that this might be my first sure-fire cure. Whereas my medical colleagues in the next room were bandaging or suturing wounds, prescribing medications, or conducting minor surgeries, it sometimes felt so futile to just listen to my patients and try to offer some reassurance. But with this boy, I was pretty sure that I'd done some measurable good, and that reinvigorated me.

My head hurt with concentration. I desperately needed a break and to use the toilet. Before I could get out of my chair, a man carried a tiny girl into the room, accompanied by a woman I assumed was the girl's mother. They were followed by the principal of the local school and Pasang Sherpa, our leader and guide.

Since confusion was my usual state of mind, I just sat and waited for the drama to unfold. I wondered what could possibly surprise me next.

"This is Pramisa," Pasang said to me, pointing to this absolutely adorable girl who was looking around the room, studying all of us carefully. "She is three years old."

I nodded, waiting. Pasang and the principal explained to me that the man and woman were her aunt and uncle.

"Where are her parents?" I asked.

Everyone looked at one another after the translation. "Her mother is at the hospital," the uncle said. "She is dressed in white."

"She is dressed in white?" I repeated, now completely confused. What did *that* have to do with anything?

"Yes," Pasang agreed. "Her husband, the girl's father, died yesterday. He was hit on the head during the last earthquake. He was in the hospital, and he died. The mother is with the body, dressed in white as she is required. This girl, she doesn't have a father, and we haven't told her yet."

I looked at this little girl, Pramisa. She was smiling and playing with a stuffed animal I had just given her. My heart just broke. I could feel myself losing control, tears running down my cheeks, and so I excused myself for a moment and walked out of the room to regain my composure. Did they think it was *my* job to tell this little girl that her father was never coming home? I had already seen and done so much, but this I could not do. But I knew I had to return the room and face them.

Once I was back in my chair, Pasang asked if we might offer this girl a scholarship and support her, now that she had lost her father and her home. They had no money, no place to live, and no way to earn an income. The mother would spend a year in mourning, and that would be her job.

I thought to myself that fate had put me in this place, at this moment in time. My chest hurt. I felt so flooded with emotion from all the accumulated stress, all the stories I had heard, all the people I had seen. I had felt so helpless at times, so inadequate to provide the help and support that everyone needed. And now I was given this gift: I could save this child, literally save her life by agreeing to provide her with a scholarship so she could have an education and a future.

I could barely speak, but I nodded my head once, twice, then up and down so vigorously that everyone looked at me curiously. "Yes, of course," I finally spoke aloud. I looked at the aunt and uncle and told them that although this was a terrible tragedy, I would do everything in my power to make certain that Pramisa was provided an education to go as far as she could in life. We would indeed help to take care of her. Then I politely excused myself and found a private place where I could compose myself.

Sara's Turn

After several more weeks of the constant pressure, thirteen-hour workdays, sleep deprivation, and my own vicarious trauma from everything I'd seen and done, I was absolute toast. My aging body was breaking down. I don't weigh much to begin with, and I'd lost so much weight my clothes were literally falling off. I needed to refuel and recover; I was no use to these people if I was too wrecked to treat them.

This visit had been among the most difficult and painful experiences of my life. Besides seeing all the devastation and suffering, I felt so disturbed, seeing so many of the girls who seemed to be giving up hope. I had known many of them most of their lives. I had spent time with their families, visiting their homes and classrooms. Now all that seemed gone as I saw them squatting in tents perched in the mud.

I knew we'd done a lot of good. I also realized that the people in Nepal are among the most resilient in the world. They'd have to be, after years of political instability and corruption, natural disasters, and government inaction, yet they *still* endured and tried to rebuild their lives. Their homes and schools had been destroyed; teachers had disappeared. They were making do with almost nothing while many of the current politicians were becoming wealthier from bribes and theft. Most people would just shrug, as if that's just the way things are, the way they'll always be. The Nepali people have taught me so much about the courage to rebuild their lives even when things appear so hopeless.

And I knew that it was time to turn operations over to Sara and others. I never enjoyed spending my time asking people for money, and I had always felt impatient navigating the complex politics of South Asia—but Sara was a master at these tasks and thrived on the challenges. At every place I visited, the children would ask about Sara and why she wasn't with me. It was pretty clear that in a remarkably short period of time, Sara had cemented deep bonds with the girls.

In order for any organization to survive, much less flourish, the original founder has to get out of the way and allow new leadership team members to impose their own vision on where they wish things to go. There was so much work to do, especially because in the coming months and years, things would continue in a downward spiral in the country. The earthquakes continued for weeks afterwards, but an even bigger problem was that with the northern border closed because of avalanches, the southern border with India remained sealed as the territorial dispute worsened. Fuel and supplies remained scarce, if nonexistent, for months afterwards. For a period of time, I remained trapped in the country just as my own health condition spiraled out of control, and I had to be hospitalized twice before I could find a flight out of the country. Out of necessity, and knowing everything Sara would be able to do, it was time for me to step aside.

Epilogue

Sara and Jeffrey
July 2016–Present

We both confess that our visits to Nepal these past few years have been among the most fulfilling, satisfying, and joyful experiences of our lives—and also the most challenging and traumatic. Each of us struggles with our own ghosts and nightmares. Friends and acquaintances we know have been seriously injured; others have died. Many are still without homes, and several have lost all hope and disappeared.

Our narrative comes to an end, but the story continues through the lives of those we have introduced to you. We hope that our efforts might demonstrate to others how relatively simple and easy it is to begin any effort designed to assist those who need help the most, whether in local communities or on a global scale. It is hardly necessary to climb a mountain or launch a foundation to get started; effort begins with identifying some cause or issue that speaks to you and then making one small gesture to begin.

Sabita, the first girl Jeffrey ever sponsored in Nepal, is now in her mid-twenties and happily married. She works as a nurse in a cancer hospital and is the first girl in her village to ever receive higher education. Sabita hopes that someday she will complete her graduate degree in public health administration.

Many of the other older girls are also now attending medical or dental school, studying at universities within Nepal and abroad. Two of the oldest girls, Seema and Radha, are pursuing medical careers in Bangladesh and plan to return to Nepal after their studies to help others. Seema hopes someday to become a neurosurgeon.

Babita, one of the first scholarship recipients, attended graduate school and completed her studies with a master's in social work from the most prestigious university in Nepal. She is now in charge of all Empower Nepali

Girls operations, handling logistics. She intends to continue her education by pursuing a law degree in order to better advocate for the girls in a system that has left them behind.

Pasang Sherpa still works as a trekking guide, among all his other community responsibilities. He is the executive in charge of the organization and oversees financial and budgeting tasks.

Chhusang Sherpa, Pasang's daughter and Jeffrey's translator during trauma missions, is attending university in the United States with a full scholarship. She someday hopes to work for the United Nations.

Jeffrey has since retired from the foundation. After the 2016 election, when immigrants and refugees in the United States and all over the world were being increasingly marginalized and neglected, he decided to devote himself to a new cause, quit his job at the university, and relocated to Houston in order to work with refugee trauma. He travels regularly to Turkey to do trainings for psychologists who work with Syrian refugees. He joined a refugee resettlement agency and medical school that focuses on helping indigent patients. He misses the children and his friends, so he returned to Nepal with Sara and a film crew to document further the courageous and resilient journeys of the girls and produce this story into a feature film.

Among the Everest team members who accompanied Sara during her fateful climb, most of them eventually summited Everest in 2017 with Damian—everyone except Kate and Sara. Each of the climbers dealt with the 2015 disaster in different ways; several experienced ongoing symptoms of post-traumatic stress, while others did their best to just move on with their lives. Sara's marriage ended just after she returned from summiting Mount Vinson, the highest mountain in Antarctica, and another one of the Seven Summits completed. Kate did not lose her fingers and plans to return to summit Everest with Sara in 2019.

Aussie Jon, one of Sara's closest friends on the climb, was a very experienced mountain climber and open-minded thinker. He recalled hanging onto the shaking ladder in the icefall with his first thoughts being about how much he loved his wife, Susan, and his sons. But that transitioned in a moment to problem-solving and action mode: What could he do to maximize his chances of survival?

Jon returned from Everest disappointed and frustrated because all that time, energy, and money had been wasted. "I hope I'm not giving you the impression that he lacked compassion or didn't have a heart," Susan explained. "Jon had a huge, loving heart, and the tragedy, the loss of life in Nepal, was hardly lost on him. More than anything, he was so grateful he made it back to us, but his disappointment about the way things turned out for him personally was a close second."

Jon made a conscious decision afterwards to reduce the risks in the future and instead chose to climb one of the easiest 8,000-meter peaks, Shisha Pangma. "Susan," he declared just before departing for Tibet, "only fourteen more months, and I'll be done." He was going to retire from dangerous climbing and spend more time with his family.

Jon was on his way to Camp One when he and a teammate, roped together, sat down to rest. A crevasse opened up below, swallowing them up. Their bodies could not be retrieved.

Hopes and Dreams

April 25, the anniversary of the earthquakes, will always be a date cemented in our memories. In some ways, nothing much has changed in Nepal. The government is still as corrupt and incompetent as ever. Much of the money donated by foreign governments or aid agencies has either disappeared, been squandered, or sits idle and wasted. There are still fuel and housing shortages, and rebuilding has taken place at an infuriatingly slow pace.

But most of the girls have tried to patch their lives back together. Some of them are now living with relatives; others have been placed in temporary housing, or we have arranged to rent rooms for them. We first began this effort so many years ago, when the cost to keep a girl in school was less than $50 per year—and that included school fees, books, uniforms, and supplies. Now that so many of the girls are older and attending institutions of higher education, the cost per girl now exceeds several thousand dollars each year for technical, medical, or nursing studies. We feel even more pressure to keep the momentum going, with so many children whose very lives depend on our efforts to help support them.

Jeffrey and Sara both faced some of their greatest fears during the events that unfolded in this story. Sara has faced so many challenges, including, of course, the fear of death but also fear of the cold, of the dark, of asking for money, of being alone, of public speaking, and of suffering. Reflecting back on all she has endured, she believes that her training and mountain climbing prepared her in ways that she could have never anticipated, especially in dealing with the breakup of her marriage.

"I have never lived my life more fully," Sara says, "than I have during this last four years. I have never felt more alive, more engaged, more passionate and excited about what I'm doing. And I can readily see how contagious this has been for others, including my family, friends, and the girls in Nepal.

"I hear so much envy from others: How can you do these things? How can you afford to do these things? How do you find the time? How do you put up with all the aggravation and difficulties? When people hear some of my stories of where I've been and what I've done, they just roll their eyes and say, 'Better you than me.' But that's not quite true.

"All my life, I have been waiting and waiting for the perfect time to do perfect things that I always wanted to do, but fear and excuses always stood in my way. I think there is no perfect time to start any new endeavor; there are always reasons to postpone. When I started mountain climbing, it was in the middle of winter, with no team or crew at the beginning, no training, no gear, no mentor, and no clear reason to do this in the first place except an impulsive gesture. But little by little, the universe gave me all that I needed and ever wanted, and even more.

"The earthquakes were absolutely tragic and devastating, but this is what we got from the universe, and I accept that. Mother Goddess Sagarmāthā, also known as Mount Everest, didn't want me up there in 2015, and I accept it fully with all my heart. It's time for me to train more and go back stronger.

"In my own way, I really did reach the top of Everest, perhaps not the mountain itself, but certainly my own summit. I was realizing an important lesson: that these climbs were not really about the destination but about the journey, the relationships I had forged with teammates and guides, and mostly about the women and children whose lives might be improved as a result of the attention I was bringing to their plight. I'm just getting started."

Facing challenges, taking risks, and tackling the things that frighten us the most are precisely the things that have most empowered us and inspired the girls to follow in our footsteps. These girls are attempting something that is absolutely unprecedented: to become the first ones in their villages to attain an education and pursue a professional career. They will become engineers, psychologists, mountaineers, or professors like us. They will demonstrate to their families and communities that they are indeed among their country's greatest resources who will someday transform their nation. That is our hope and dream.

Acknowledgments

None of our work, or our adventures, could have been possible without our many friends and family members who have tolerated our long absences while working abroad or climbing mountains in faraway places.

We are most grateful to Pasang Temba Sherpa, Babita Gurung, A. D. Sherpa, John Child, Funuru Sherpa, Kumar Bhattarai, Chhusang Sherpa, and the dozens of Nepali volunteers who assist us with our collective work creating opportunities for girls and young women who would not otherwise have a chance for an education.

Finally, Jeffrey is most grateful for the love and constant support of his wife, Ellen, who has been far more than a cheerleader but also an active partner in our mission.

About the Authors

Sara Safari is an author, speaker, mountain climber, advocate for women's empowerment, and board member of Empower Nepali Girls. In 2015, she received the prestigious Global Citizen Award from the United Nations in recognition of her humanitarian work with Nepali girls and her continued efforts to end human trafficking. She's also received the International Leadership Association's Outstanding Practice with Broad Impact award in the area of women and leadership. Sara will be the first Iranian in history to climb the Seven Summits, the seven highest peaks on each continent/ She is climbing on behalf of women worldwide who don't have the opportunity to live their lives fully expressed and on their own terms.

Jeffrey Kottler is an impassioned humanitarian and the founder of Empower Nepali Girls, a nonprofit that protects and mentors lower-caste Nepali girls, a group at great risk of being forced into early marriage or sold into sex slavery. For the past forty-five years, he has worked as a psychologist and educator in mental health centers, nongovernmental organizations (NGO), and disaster relief settings. Jeffrey is a clinical professor of psychiatry at Baylor College of Medicine in Houston. He is the author of over one hundred nonfiction books including: *On Being a Therapist, Living and Being a Therapist: Selected Writings of Jeffrey Kottler, What You Don't Know About Leadership But Probably Should: Applications to Daily Life, and Change: What Leads to Personal Transformation.*